4

W9-BSY-835

Concepts & Comments

Third Edition

Patricia Ackert | Linda Lee

THOMSON

HEINLE

Australia   Canada   Mexico   Singapore   United Kingdom   United States

THOMSON
HEINLE

Reading & Vocabulary Development 4: Concepts & Comments, Third Edition
Patricia Ackert and Linda Lee

Publisher, Adult and Academic ESL:
James W. Brown
Senior Acquisitions Editor: Sherrise Roehr
Director of Product Development: Anita Raducanu
Development Editor: Tom Jefferies
Editorial Assistant: Katherine Reilly
Director of Product Marketing: Amy Mabley
Product Marketing Manager: Laura Needham
Senior Field Marketing Manager: Donna Lee Kennedy

Senior Production Editor: Maryellen E. Killeen
Senior Print Buyer: Mary Beth Hennebury
Compositor: Pre-Press Company, Inc.
Project Manager: Sally Lifland, Lifland et al., Bookmakers
Photo Researcher: Gail Magin
Cover Designer: Ha Ngyuen
Text Designer: Quica Ostrander
Printer: Quebecor/World

Copyright © 2005 by Thomson Heinle, a part of The Thomson Corporation. Thomson, the star logo and Heinle are trademarks used herein under license.

All rights reserved. No part of this work covered by the copyright hereon may be reproduced or used in any form or by any means—graphic, electronic, or mechanical, including photocopying, recording, taping, Web distribution or information storage and retrieval systems—without the written permission of the publisher.

CNN. Trademark and Copyright 2004 Cable News Network LP, LLLP. A Time Warner Company. All Rights Reserved. Licensed by Turner Learning, Inc. A Time Warner Company. All Rights Reserved.

Printed in the United States of America
1 2 3 4 5 6 7 8 9 10   09 08 07 06 05

For more information contact Thomson Heinle, 25 Thomson Place, Boston, Massachusetts 02210 USA, or you can visit our Internet site at elt.thomson.com

For permission to use material from this text or product contact us:

Tel	1-800-730-2214
Fax	1-800-730-2215
Web	www.thomsonrights.com

ISBN: 1-4130-0417-2
ISE ISBN: 1-4130-0448-2

Library of Congress Control Number: 2005932285

Contents

To the Instructor

Reading & Vocabulary Development 4: Concepts & Comments is a best-selling reading skills text designed for students of English as a second or foreign language who have a basic vocabulary in English of about 2,000 words. This text teaches about 500 more words.

Concepts & Comments is one in a series of reading skills texts. The complete series has been designed to meet the needs of students from the beginning to the high intermediate levels and includes the following:

Reading & Vocabulary Development 1: Facts & Figures
Reading & Vocabulary Development 2: Thoughts & Notions
Reading & Vocabulary Development 3: Cause & Effect
Reading & Vocabulary Development 4: Concepts & Comments

Concepts & Comments is a brand-new addition to the *Reading & Vocabulary Development* series. Previously published as a low-intermediate text, *Concepts & Comments* has been comprehensively revised for students at the high-intermediate level. Building on the strengths of the other books in the series, *Concepts & Comments* balances engaging readings with systematic recycling of reading, vocabulary, and grammar skills.

Methodology of *Concepts & Comments*

Concepts & Comments uses the following methodology:

• **Theme-based approach to reading.** Each of the five units has a theme: art, organizations, places, science and technology, and health and well-being.

• **Systematic presentation and recycling of vocabulary.** One of the primary tasks of students is developing a useful and personally relevant vocabulary base. In *Concepts & Comments*, up to 24 words are introduced in each lesson. These words appear in boldface type. Those underlined are glossed in the margin. All of the new vocabulary items are used several times in the lesson, and then are systematically recycled throughout the text.

• **Pedagogical design.** The central goal of *Concepts & Comments* is to help students develop the critical reading skills they will need for academic, personal, and/or career purposes. By any standard, the range of exercise types in *Concepts & Comments* is rich and varied. This text provides students with practice in comprehension, building vocabulary, making inferences, finding the main idea, determining cause and effect, scanning, summarizing, paraphrasing, understanding the sequence of events, and learning to work more effectively with two-word verbs, compound words, connecting words, and noun substitutes.

Organization of *Concepts & Comments*

Concepts & Comments is organized into five units. Each unit contains four lessons packed with exercises and activities.

• **"Before You Read" Questions.** These pre-reading questions provide a motivation for reading the text.

• **Context Clues.** A context clue exercise at the beginning of each lesson introduces some of the vocabulary for the following lesson. This section is designed to pre-teach particularly important vocabulary items.

• **Vocabulary.** The first two exercises give practice with new words in a different context but with the same meaning.

• **Vocabulary Review.** Vocabulary items are used in subsequent texts and exercises to give additional review. They are fill-ins or matching synonyms and antonyms.

• **Comprehension.** First is a set of true/false/not enough information or multiple choice questions. Then come comprehension questions, which include inference and discussion questions. The comprehension questions may also be given as written assignments.

• **NEW! Reading Strategy.** Students acquire important academic reading skills such as the ability to take notes, make inferences, and understand cause and effect. These skills are recycled throughout the text.

• **Vocabulary Expansion.** Through collocation, word form, and prefix/suffix activities, each lesson encourages students to expand on the vocabulary they have learned.

• **Grammar.** A selection of grammar exercises at the end of each lesson reinforces structural points from the readings. These exercises include work with noun substitutes, articles, compound nouns, and verb tenses.

• **Writing.** Each lesson closes with a writing exercise.

• **Extension Activities.** Each unit ends with a set of high-interest, interactive tasks to help students practice the new vocabulary and the skills they have learned in more open-ended contexts.

CNN® Video Highlights—The highlight of each set of extension activities is a short video-based lesson centered on a stimulating, authentic clip from the CNN® video archives. Each video lesson follows the same sequence of activities:

Before You Watch encourages students to recall background knowledge based on their own experiences or from information presented in the readings.

As You Watch asks students to watch for general information such as the topic of the clip.

After You Watch gets the students to expand on the main points of the video by establishing further connections to the reading passages, their own experiences, and their ideas and opinions.

Activity Page—The crossword puzzles found on this page encourage students to practice the vocabulary found in each unit.

Dictionary Page—Exercises on this page offer students practice with dictionary skills based on entries from *The Newbury House Dictionary of American English.*

• **Skills Index.** This index provides teachers and students with a handy reference for all of the reading and writing skills introduced in *Concepts & Comments,* as well as all of the grammatical structures found in the text.

 ## Supplements for *Concepts & Comments*

Concepts & Comments has a full suite of student and instructor supplements.

• A complete Answer Key provides answers to all the exercises in the student book.

• Authentic CNN® video clips for each unit are included in VHS and DVD formats. Transcripts for the clips appear in the Answer Key.

• Audio cassettes and CD's include all the readings from the text.

• *ExamView® Pro* test-generating software allows instructors to create custom tests and quizzes.

• A new website (found at http://elt.thomson.com/ readingandvocabulary) features vocabulary flashcards, crossword puzzles, quizzes, and more to help students review for tests.

Acknowledgments

The authors and publisher would like to thank the following individuals who offered helpful feedback and suggestions for the revision of the *Reading & Vocabulary Development* series:

Brian Altano—Bergen Community College, Paramus, NJ

Benjamin Deleon—Delano High School, Delano, CA

Elaine Dow—Quinsigamond Community College, Worcester, MA

Julia Karet—Chaffey College, Rancho Cucamonga, CA

Jane Sitko—Edmonds Community College, Lynnwood, WA

ix

*Every child is an artist. The problem is how to
remain an artist once [you] grow up.*
—Pablo Picasso

© Jeff Greenberg/Photo Edit

Navajo Sand Painting

© Ted Spiegel/CORBIS

Before You Read

1. What three adjectives would you use to describe the sand painting in the photograph?

2. How do you think a sand painting is made?

3. Sand paintings are usually destroyed soon after they are finished. Why do you think this is done?

Context Clues

It is not necessary to look up every new word in the dictionary. Often, the other words and ideas in the sentence or surrounding sentences (the context) can help you guess the meaning of the new word. When you are reading, try to use context to guess the meaning of new words. Try not to look up every new word in your dictionary.

*The words in **bold** print below are from this lesson. Use context clues to guess what each word means. Do all of the Context Clues exercises in the book this way.*

1. More than 500 years ago, the **ancestors** of the Navajo people moved south.

2. A small sand painting may have 2 or 3 people working on it, while a large painting may **require** 10 people.

3. At the end of the ceremony, it is **imperative** that the sand painting be destroyed. The Navajo believe that something terrible will happen if they don't do this.

4. One reason for this change is the **extensive** training necessary to perform the duties of a singer; it can take as long as 14 years to train someone.

5. A singer can train only one student at a time. This need for **one-on-one** training has limited the number of students who can be trained.

1 Navajo Sand Painting

More than 500 years ago, the **ancestors** of the Navajo people left the cold northern region that is now part of western Canada and Alaska and migrated south to what is now the southwestern part of the United States.

5 The area in which the Navajo finally settled is **mainly** desert. It is a **harsh** environment that gets little rain. The animals and plants that live there have had to **adapt** in order to survive in the **unforgiving** climate and **landscape.**

mostly; primarily

10 When the Navajo arrived in the area, they too had to adapt to the harsh desert conditions in order to survive. They had to learn to make use of the natural resources in their environment to provide for their shelter, food, and other necessities. Over time, the Navajo became

15 famous for the things they were able to create from the natural resources at hand. One of the most famous Navajo creations is called sand painting.

Most people think of a painting as a work of art. For the Navajo, however, sand painting is not artwork.

20 Rather, sand painting is an important part of a religious ceremony. The making of a sand painting is part of a **healing** ceremony that is supposed to **restore** the health and **well-being** of a sick person.

bring back; return to normal

good mental and physical condition

The only people who are allowed to create sand

25 paintings are specially trained Navajo "singers" or "medicine men" and their **assistants**. A Navajo singer begins the process of creating a sand painting by collecting different rocks. The rocks are then crushed and ground into sand. Traditionally, a Navajo singer

30 and his assistants make the sand painting on the floor of a small Navajo house called a *hogan*. Working under the direction of the singer, the assistants take colored sand in their hands and drip it on the floor in a line. Using different colors, they slowly make a picture.

35 The size of Navajo sand paintings varies. A small sand painting is less than a meter wide, while a large

sand painting can be over 6 meters wide. The number of people assisting the singer also varies. A small sand painting may have 2 or 3 people working on it and take
40 an hour to complete, while a large painting may **require** 10 men and women and take all day to finish.

During the healing ceremony, the sick person moves onto the completed sand painting. The sick person sits directly on the sand painting so that it can **serve** as a
45 pathway for **evil** or illness to leave the person's body and for goodness or health to return to it. This explains why the Navajo word for sand painting means "place where the gods come and go." After the sick person has been treated, other visitors may go up to the painting and dab
50 some of the sand on themselves so that the sand painting brings health and well-being into their lives too.

At the end of the healing ceremony, it is **imperative** that the sand painting be destroyed. The Navajo believe that something terrible will happen if they fail to
55 destroy a sand painting **properly**. So, in the reverse of   **correctly** the order in which it was made, the singer sweeps the painting away and returns the sand to the landscape.

Navajo singers make their sand paintings from memory, and they always make the same pictures in
60 exactly the same way. There are between 600 and 1,000 different pictures for sand paintings. At one point in history, there was one singer for every 150 Navajos. Today, the **ratio** is much lower, with one singer for   **relationship between two numbers** roughly every 2,200 people. One reason for this change
65 is the **extensive** training required to perform the duties of a singer; it can take as long as 14 years to train someone. A second reason for the change in ratio is that a singer can train only one student at a time. This need for **one-on-one** training has limited the number of
70 students who can be trained.

While a true sand painting is part of a Navajo ceremony and lasts for only a short time, sand painting as a permanent art form has also developed. The first permanent sand paintings appeared in the early 1900s.
75 These early pieces of art were actually **tapestries** rather   **artworks made of cloth, often used as wall hangings**

than paintings made with sand. The tapestries were **woven** by a **respected** Navajo singer named Hosteen Klah, who copied the pictures from sand paintings. However, to avoid causing something terrible to

80 happen by making a permanent picture, Klah never made the picture exactly the same as the **original**. He would not use a Navajo picture without changing it a little. Before long, tourists in the area saw Klah's weavings and asked to buy them. Klah finally agreed to

85 sell one of his weavings if the buyer **promised** never to put it on the floor or walk on it.

In the 1930s, the Navajo began creating another type of permanent sand painting. They made these permanent paintings by slowly dripping colored sand

90 onto glue-covered boards. Today, these sand paintings are considered to be works of art rather than part of a religious ceremony. They are made by artists rather than singers, and they appear in art shows and in art museums.

95 There is still **controversy** over the selling of sand paintings. Some Navajos say that sand paintings are part of their religion and should not be sold. But others believe that the artists' changes to the pictures protect their religious power.

made from yarn into cloth; past participle of *weave*

admired

a   Vocabulary

In this book, difficult words are repeated several times in the exercises. These words are also repeated and reviewed in other lessons. It is not necessary to list new English words with their meanings in your own language. You will learn them just by practicing.

In the Vocabulary exercises in this book, write the correct word in each blank. Use a word only once, and use capital letters if they are necessary.

harshly	ratio	proper	controversy
one-on-one	original	tapestries	ancestors
assistant	landscape	evil	well-being

1. The _____ way to destroy a sand painting is to sweep it away.

2. To become a Navajo singer, a person needs _____ training, or private instruction.

3. People have different likes and dislikes. That's why there is always _____ about what makes good art.

4. There are 10 men and 5 women in a class. That's a _____ of 2 to 1.

5. The _____ in some parts of the country is mountainous.

6. You should make a copy of your birth certificate and then put the _____ in a safe place.

7. I apologize for speaking to you _____, but I was very angry.

8. He can't do all the research by himself. He really needs an _____.

9. You can be certain that our _____ lived very differently from the way we live now.

10. Parents are always concerned about the _____ of their children.

11. The Navajo believe that a sand painting can help to drive _____ out of a person.

12. Navajo _____ are very expensive, but they look beautiful hanging on a wall.

b Vocabulary

Do this exercise the same way you did Exercise a.

adapt	heal	restore	require
serve	imperative	weave	extensively
respect	promises	mainly	unforgiving

1. How long would it take you to _____ to a completely different environment?

2. In some cultures, shaking hands when you meet someone is a sign of _____ .

3. You can't depend on people who break their _____; you can never be sure they will do what they say they will do.

4. If you cut yourself, you should clean the cut so that it can _____ properly.

5. To get a driver's license, it is _____ that you learn the rules of the road.

6. Before he could write his report, he had to study the topic _____ .

7. A loom is a frame or a machine that is used to _____ cloth and tapestries.

8. Their house is made _____ of wood, but there is a little stonework on the front.

9. A piece of woven material can _____ as a wall hanging or a rug.

10. He tried many different things to _____ his health.

11. Did your parents _____ you to help out with the cooking and cleaning at home?

12. An _____ person never lets you forget the things you did wrong; an _____ climate never lets you forget how harsh it is.

c Comprehension Check: True/False/Not Enough Information

*Write **T** if the sentence is true, **F** if it is false, and **NI** if there is not enough information in the text to answer the question. Change the false sentences to make them true, or explain why they are false. Do all the True/False/Not Enough Information exercises in the lessons this way.*

_____ 1. Sand paintings play a role in Navajo religious ceremonies.

_____ 2. Navajo sand paintings are usually created by a "singer," who paints a picture on a wall.

_____ 3. The ancestors of the Navajo made sand paintings.

_____ 4. Most sand paintings are very small, measuring less than a meter wide.

_____ 5. The purpose of a sand painting is to help someone who is ill become well.

_____ 6. During a healing ceremony, no one can touch the sand painting.

_____ 7. Many Navajos believe that something bad will happen if they don't destroy a sand painting correctly.

_____ 8. Navajo singers never paint pictures of the same things; every picture is very different.

_____ 9. It is quite difficult to become a Navajo singer.

_____ 10. Today, many tourists participate in Navajo religious ceremonies.

d Comprehension Questions

Answer these questions in complete sentences.

1. Where did the Navajo's ancestors come from?
2. What happens during a Navajo healing ceremony?
3. How is a traditional sand painting made?
4. What happens to a sand painting after the healing ceremony?
5. Why are there so few Navajo singers today?
6. What role did Hosteen Klah play in the development of sand painting as an art form?
7. How are the sand paintings in museums different from the sand paintings used in healing ceremonies?

Reading Strategy: Taking Notes in a Chart

It often helps to take notes as you read. Taking notes can help you to understand and remember what you read. One simple way to take notes is in a T-chart like the one below.

On the left side of the chart, you'll find the topic of each of the first six paragraphs. On the right side, write the main idea.

Topic	Main idea
the migration of the ancestors of the Navajo	*They moved to what is now the southwestern United States.*
adapting to desert life	
the purpose of a sand painting	
making a sand painting	
the size of a sand painting	
the healing ceremony	

 Vocabulary Expansion: Word Forms

Choose the right word form for each sentence below. Use a word from line 1 in sentence 1, and so on. You may have to change the verb form or make the noun plural.

	Verb	Noun	Adjective	Adverb
1.	adapt	adaptation	adaptable	
2.	heal	healer	healing	
3.	restore	restoration	restorative	
4.	require	requirement	required	
5.	reverse	reversal		
6.	extend	extension	extensive	extensively
7.		controversy	controversial	
8.	weave	weaving	woven	
9.	respect	respect	respectful	respectfully
10.	originate	origin	original	originally

10

1. He wasn't able to _____ to the living conditions here, and so he returned home.
2. A medical doctor is a trained _____.
3. When you are tired from working hard, a vacation can be

    _____.
4. What are the _____ for becoming a Navajo singer?
5. First she drove the car forward, and then she _____ direction and drove backward.
6. To get a PhD, you have to do _____ research.
7. In the United States, the issue of who should own a gun is very

    _____.
8. His parents taught him how to _____.
9. She was taught to speak _____ to her grandparents.
10. _____ I wanted to be a pilot, but later I decided to become an artist.

g Grammar Review: Articles

*Put an article (**the, a,** or **an**) in each blank if one is needed.*

1. More than 500 years ago, _____ ancestors of _____ Navajo people left _____ cold northern region that is now _____ part of _____ western Canada and _____ Alaska.
2. Most people think of _____ painting as _____ work of art.
3. Sand painting is _____ important part of _____ religious ceremony.
4. The size of _____ Navajo sand paintings varies. _____ small sand painting is less than a meter wide, while _____ large sand painting can be over 6 meters wide.
5. Today, these sand paintings are considered to be _____ works of art rather than part of _____ religious ceremony. They are made by _____ artists rather than singers, and they appear in _____ art shows and in _____ art museums.

h Sentence Combining

Read the example and the model combinations below. Then rewrite sentences 1 and 2 following the models.

Example: The ancestors of the Navajo migrated south. They eventually settled in a desert area.

Models: a. The ancestors of the Navajo migrated south, and they eventually settled in a desert area.
b. The ancestors of the Navajo migrated south and eventually settled in a desert area.
c. The ancestors of the Navajo migrated south, eventually settling in a desert area.

1. The Navajo singer sweeps the sand painting away. Then he returns the sand to the landscape.

    a. _____

    b. _____

    c. _____

2. Sick people sit on the sand paintings. They wait for the illness to leave their bodies.

    a. _____

    b. _____

    c. _____

i Writing

Every culture has its own kinds of art. What is a traditional art form in your culture? Write a paragraph about a traditional art form from your culture. If you can, bring a picture to class to show an example of this kind of art. When you finish, exchange paragraphs with a partner.

2   Ceramics

The most ancient **artifacts** in our **possession** today were made out of clay many thousands of years ago. **In fact**, much of what we now know about cultures of the past we learned by studying pieces of their clay dishes
5 and clay figures. Very few things made from other **materials** have survived to tell us about the cultures that produced them.

human-made objects of historical interest

ownership

Objects made from clay came to be called ceramics from the Greek word *keramos*, which means "potter's
10 clay." Ceramics are divided into many different kinds based on the type of clay used and how the clay is **fired**. The most common types of ceramics are pottery, stoneware, and porcelain. To make pottery, for example, clay is fired at about 500°C. Clay fired at about 1200°C
15 becomes stoneware. When white clay is fired at an even higher temperature, it becomes porcelain. Baking the clay at such high temperatures actually changes the **structure** of the clay so that it becomes permanently hard and almost **indestructible**.

the way something is put together

20 The art of making pottery developed in many places around the world. Some of the earliest pieces of pottery were probably made when people tried to strengthen baskets woven of grass and sticks. Some archeologists think that early potters in China may have covered the
25 inside of woven baskets with clay so that the baskets would hold water. When the baskets were either placed on a fire or left there by mistake, the fire burned the grass away and turned the baskets into hard, **durable** pots.

long-lasting

30 Early potters in different parts of the world found interesting ways to **decorate** their work to make it more attractive. They **scratched** the surface of the soft clay to make decorative lines and designs. They also used glazes, which are a special kind of paint, to make clay
35 objects smooth, shiny, and colorful. The Egyptians were already decorating their pottery with colors and designs

15

about 5,000 years ago. Similar **styles** began to **spread** throughout the Mediterranean region. By 3,500 years ago, the people of the Greek island of Crete were

40 producing their own pottery decorated with designs and images of animals. These designs survived thousands of years and can still be seen in examples of ancient Greek art.

The pottery makers of China were the first to learn

45 to make porcelain, which is the **finest** and most **fragile** type of pottery. If you hold a piece of porcelain up in the air, light will shine through it. The Chinese exported porcelain to Europe, where it became highly valued. For many years, European potters tried to copy Chinese

50 porcelain, but it was not until 1710 that a German scientist finally learned how to make it. By the end of the 18th century, other European countries were also producing porcelain, and today France and England produce some of the finest porcelain in the world.

55 There are different ways to form a clay dish or bowl. The easiest method is to simply hollow out a clay ball, using your hands. Another simple method is to roll the clay into a long "rope" and then **wind** it into a shape. A third method is to spread the clay around something.

60 The invention of the potter's wheel more than 5,000 years ago introduced an **entirely** new way to form a clay object. With this method, the potter places some clay in the center of a round, flat wheel that can turn very fast. As the wheel turns, the potter uses his or her

65 hands to shape the clay. Using a potter's wheel makes it possible to form clay objects that are smoother and more **uniformly** round.

A clay object is usually decorated first and then baked. Baking the clay at very high temperatures makes

70 it hard and strong. Firing also makes the glaze stick to the pottery. When the firing is completed, the potter must carefully remove the pottery from the oven and let it cool slowly. If it cools too quickly, it could **crack** and break.

75 Over the years, clay objects have served many **purposes**. Obviously, one of the most common uses of

make into a circular shape (around something)

completely

evenly; the same all around

pottery is for household dishes. Because pottery is strong and waterproof, it makes an excellent dish for carrying, storing, cooking, and serving food. Fired clay
80 has also been used to make bricks for building houses and to make tiles for covering floors. Ceramics are also **<u>incredibly</u>** heat **resistant**, so they can be used where metal would melt or become weak. Today, ceramics are important in industry and engineering.

very; extremely

85   One rarely discussed use of ceramics is for burial ceremonies. In some cultures, special ceramic objects were buried along with the dead person. Archeologists think these ceramic objects were made especially for burial ceremonies because their decoration is elaborate.
90 In some cultures, parts of a dead person's body were removed, placed in ceramic vases, and then buried with the body. Ceramic objects showing a dead person's title and offices held have also been found at burial sites.

    Some people refuse to consider the making of
95 ceramics an art form because the objects created are so often useful things. At the same time, however, many of those useful ceramic things are extremely valuable. Some are even kept in museums. In the country of Iran, ancient pottery is considered to be so valuable to the
100 culture that there are harsh **punishments** for anyone who tries to take ceramic artifacts out of the country. The punishments range from paying money to time in **jail**. That is certainly a clear indication that ceramics are valued by many people.

a Vocabulary

Write the correct word in each blank. Use a word only once, and use capital letters if they are necessary.

fired	scratch	wind	spread
resist	punishment	crack	artifacts
possessions	durable	structure	decorate

1. Many _____ from ancient cultures are kept in museums.
2. You can use a glaze to _____ a piece of pottery.
3. There is a serious _____ for stealing ancient artifacts.
4. Ceramics are more _____ than tapestries.
5. Ceramics are _____ in a special kind of oven called a kiln.
6. You can use your fingernail to _____ a word into clay.
7. During the war, many people put their most valuable _____ into a suitcase and left the city.
8. When you are very hungry, it's difficult to _____ eating something.
9. The bowl wasn't worth much because it had a long _____ in it.
10. Do you _____ anything on your bread before you eat it?
11. I need to work on the _____ of my paper; it is not clear how the ideas fit together.
12. They tried to _____ the cloth around his leg to stop the cut from bleeding.

b Vocabulary

Do this exercise the same way you did Exercise a.

indestructible	style	finest	fragile
punish	entire	uniform	purpose
incredible	jail	materials	in fact

1. People have been decorating pottery for a long time. _____, the Egyptians were making designs on their pottery about 5,000 years ago.

2. Machine-made dishes are more _____ than hand-made ones.

3. If you drop something _____, it will break.

4. Do you know what _____ are used to make porcelain?

5. The _____ restaurant in town is also the most expensive.

6. His story is _____. I just can't believe it.

7. Did your parents ever _____ you by sending you to bed without dinner?

8. My grandmother spent her _____ life in California. She never lived anywhere else.

9. In the 1970s, a funny _____ of pants with wide legs at the bottom was popular.

10. If you break a law, you might have to go to _____.

11. What is your _____ for studying English?

12. Something that is almost _____ will last for a very long time.

C Comprehension Check: True/False/Not Enough Information

*Write **T** if the sentence is true, **F** if it is false, and **NI** if there is not enough information in the text to answer the question. Change the false sentences to make them true, or explain why they are false.*

_____ 1. Plates and bowls are examples of pottery.

_____ 2. The word *ceramics* comes from the Greek word for "potter's clay."

_____ 3. The earliest forms of pottery were made in Crete about 7,000 years ago.

_____ 4. Porcelain is made from hard, red clay.

_____ 5. There is only one way to shape clay.

_____ 6. The Germans invented porcelain.

_____ 7. Pottery is more fragile than porcelain.

_____ 8. The Chinese invented pottery.

_____ 9. Metal is more heat resistant than ceramics.

_____ 10. Today, ceramics have few uses in industry and building.

d Comprehension Questions

Answer these questions in complete sentences.

1. What are ceramics?
2. What are ceramics used for?
3. Why are clay pots baked, or fired?
4. What are Chinese potters famous for?
5. What is the difference between pottery and porcelain?
6. How does a potter shape the clay?
7. What can we learn from the decoration on ancient pottery?
8. Do you think the making of ceramics is an art form? Why or why not?

e Reading Strategy: Distinguishing Facts and Opinions

When you read, it's important to distinguish facts from opinions. A fact is something known to be true, while an opinion is what someone believes or thinks is true.

*Identify each statement below as a fact or an opinion. Write **Fact** or **Opinion** on the line preceding each sentence.*

_____ 1. Some of the earliest pieces of pottery were probably made when people tried to strengthen baskets woven of grass and sticks.

_____ 2. Some archeologists think that early potters in China may have covered the inside of woven baskets with clay so that the baskets would hold water.

_____ 3. By about 3,500 years ago, the people of the Greek island of Crete were producing their own pottery decorated with designs and images of animals.

_____ 4. The pottery makers of China were the first to learn to make porcelain.

_____ 5. Baking the clay at very high temperatures makes it hard and strong.

20

_____ 6. Archeologists think some ceramic objects were made especially for burial ceremonies because their decoration is elaborate.

_____ 7. Ceramic objects showing a dead person's title and offices held have been found at burial sites.

f Vocabulary Expansion: Multiple Meanings

Study the different meanings of each word below. Then read the sentences and choose the correct meaning for the word as it is used in each sentence. Write the letter of the definition on the line preceding each sentence.

wind
a *noun* the natural movement of air outdoors
b *verb* to wrap around
c *verb* to turn and tighten

_____ 1. The line of people in front of the store is so long that it winds around the corner.

_____ 2. There is a strong wind outside today.

_____ 3. You can wind a clock or a watch.

fine
a *noun* money paid as a punishment for wrongdoing
b *verb* to order payment for wrongdoing
c *adjective* excellent

_____ 4. That's a fine piece of pottery.

_____ 5. The police fined him for driving too fast.

_____ 6. If the police catch you speeding, you will have to pay a fine.

uniform
a *noun* a special type of clothing worn by members of an organization
b *adjective* the same throughout

_____ 7. In most countries, the police wear uniforms.

_____ 8. When the height of the trees is uniform, they make a straight line.

g Grammar Review: Prepositions

*Complete the paragraphs with the correct prepositions (**about, in, from, of, for, or to**).*

The most ancient artifacts (1) _____ our possession today were made out (2) _____ clay many thousands (3) _____ years ago. In fact, much (4) _____ what we now know about cultures (5) _____ the past we learned by studying their clay dishes and clay figures. Very few things made (6) _____ other materials have survived to tell us (7) _____ the cultures that produced them.

Some people refuse to consider the making (8) _____ ceramics an art form because the objects created are so often useful things. At the same time, however, many useful ceramic things are extremely valuable. Some are even kept (9) _____ museums. In the country (10) _____ Iran, pottery is considered to be so valuable to the culture that there are harsh punishments (11) _____ anyone who tries to take ceramic artifacts out (12) _____ the country. The punishments range (13) _____ paying money (14) _____ jail or even death.

h Sentence Combining

Read the example and the model combinations below. Then rewrite sentences 1 to 3 following the models.

Example: You can make pottery with clay. You heat it to about 500°C.

Models: a. To make pottery, you heat clay to about 500°C.
           b. You can make pottery by heating clay to about 500°C.
           c. Pottery is made by heating clay to about 500°C.

1. You can make porcelain with white clay. You heat it to a very high temperature.

a. _____

b. _____

c. _____

2. You can make a cake with flour, eggs, sugar, and milk. You mix everything together and bake it for an hour.

   a. _____

   b. _____

   c. _____

3. A smoothie is a drink made of fruit, such as bananas and strawberries. You can make a smoothie by mixing the fruit in a blender.

   a. _____

   b. _____

   c. _____

i Writing

Write about one of your possessions. Describe it, tell how you got it, and explain why it is important to you.

lesson 3   Cave Paintings

© Bettmann/CORBIS

Before You Read

1. How old do you think this painting is?

2. What kind of animal is shown in the painting?

3. What does the painting tell you about the place where it was found?

Context Clues

*The words in **bold** print below are from this lesson. Use context clues to guess what each word means.*

1. On December 18, they **noticed** the half-covered entrance to an unnamed cave. Even though it didn't look like a very interesting cave, Eliette Deschamps pushed herself through the small opening.

2. The three explorers returned to their truck to get a **ladder**, and even though it was already dark, they decided to go down into the cave.

3. Many of the paintings are very detailed. **For instance**, several of the pictures of lions show the varied patterns of spots on their faces.

4. When Jean Clottes was asked about the cave paintings, he said, "I was deeply **moved** when I saw the paintings. They're as good as any art made anywhere in the world."

3   Cave Paintings

In December 1994, three **amateur** cave explorers—
Jean-Marie Chauvet, Eliette Brunel Deschamps, and
Christian Hillaire—were investigating an area in
southeastern France. On December 18, they **noticed** the

5 half-covered entrance to an unnamed cave. **Although** it
didn't look like a very interesting cave, Eliette
Deschamps pushed herself through the small opening.
To her surprise, she saw a huge cave below. The three
explorers returned to their truck to get a **ladder**, and

10 even though it was already dark, they decided to go
down into the cave. Once there, they discovered a **vast**
network of rooms. On the walls were some of the most
beautiful paintings they had ever seen.

The cave discovered on December 18, 1994, is now

15 called Chauvet Cave, after one of the amateur explorers

not professional; doing something for fun, not as a job

even though

very large; enormous

who discovered it. Archeologists who inspected the cave paintings soon after they were discovered estimated that the paintings were about 17,000 years old. A few months later, however, tests showed that
20 three of the animals in the paintings were at least 31,000 years old. That **meant** the paintings in Chauvet Cave were the oldest existing cave paintings in the world.

There are more than 300 paintings in Chauvet Cave. Seventy-three of the paintings are of a type of lion that
25 is now extinct. Other paintings show panthers, horses, mammoths, wooly rhinoceros, and other animals. There are also __tracings__ of human hands as well as symbols such as dots forming a __semicircle__.

copies made by drawing around something

half of a circle

Many of the paintings are __extraordinarily__ detailed.
30 __For instance__, several of the pictures of lions show the varied patterns of whisker spots that biologists today use to **identify** individual animals. The artists used the natural **curves** of the cave walls to make the animals look real. They used **shading** and color (black, red, and
35 yellow) to add depth to their paintings. When the French archeologist Jean Clottes was asked about the cave paintings, he said, "I was deeply **moved** when I saw the paintings. They're as good as any art made anywhere in the world."

extremely; very

for example

40 The paintings in Chauvet Cave were most likely done by a number of artists. Some of the paintings are extraordinarily __sophisticated__. With simple lines and shading, the artists created __exquisite__ pictures of wild animals __in action__. Some of the paintings, however, are
45 __stiff__ and stylized, and others are quite __rough__ and amateurish. Some archeologists have suggested that the painters worked with assistants. Perhaps the assistants made the rough paintings while trying to copy their teachers' paintings.

complex

perfectly made

moving; doing something

not showing movement well

not very high quality

50 When the paintings in Chauvet Cave were discovered, they were perfectly **preserved** on the stone walls. No sunlight had entered the cave from the time the paintings were made until Chauvet and his friends found them. Unfortunately, the simple act of **exposing**
55 paintings so that people can see them can cause the

26

paintings to disappear. This happened to the paintings in another cave—within six months of the opening of the cave, the paintings had vanished. Now scientists know that they must enter caves carefully and prevent
60 light and air from damaging the pictures. Today, Chauvet Cave is closed to the public, because even the breathing of a large number of people could damage the paintings.

Perhaps the most interesting thing about Chauvet
65 Cave is that it has forced archeologists to change their ideas about art. For many years, archeologists believed that it took thousands of years for humans to gradually learn how to draw and paint. Chauvet Cave showed that there were great artists 30,000 years ago. Jean
70 Clottes summed it up, saying, "Our ancestors did not need **millennia** of <u>**trial and error**</u> to achieve great art. Artistic capacity was one of the <u>**components**</u> of our species probably right from the start."

experimentation; testing

parts

Chauvet Cave is only one of many caves in the
75 world that have been decorated by ancient paintings. In Australia, South Africa, China and many other places, extraordinary ancient works of art have been found. Why did prehistoric people make these paintings? Perhaps they believed that painting the animals gave
80 the artists special strength or powers. Perhaps the paintings were part of a ceremony, or perhaps they were thought to hold some sort of magic. The answer to this question will probably always remain a mystery.

a   Vocabulary

amateur	ladder	exquisite	trial and error
tracing	identify	curve	semicircle
stiff	rough	preserved	millennium

1. On January, 1, 2000, a new _____ started.

2. Edison experimented with many different materials while trying to invent the light bulb. After years of _____, he was finally successful.

3. You can use a _____ to get up to the roof of the house.

4. A professional athlete earns money for playing a sport, while an _____ athlete does not.

5. When you are driving a car, you should slow down when you come to a sharp _____ in the road.

6. One way to make a copy of something is to make a _____.

7. Before people had refrigerators, they _____ their food in jars.

8. Half of a circle is a _____.

9. If you sleep on an uncomfortable bed, your back might feel _____ in the morning.

10. When you write something, it's a good idea to write a _____ draft first, just to get your ideas down on paper.

11. Do you know how to _____ an original Navajo tapestry?

12. The archeologists found an _____ vase buried in the ground; it must be very valuable.

b   Vocabulary

notice	components	vast	extraordinarily
moved	means	for instance	sophisticated
expose	in action	although	shading

1. The word *durable* _____ long-lasting.

2. Unlike a pond or a lake, an ocean is _____.

3. In very cold weather, it's not a good idea to _____ your hands to the cold air.
4. Did you _____ how many people were in the room?
5. Only a very cold person would not be _____ by the pictures of the disaster.
6. Einstein was an _____ intelligent person.
7. _____ the paintings were made thousands of years ago, they are still in very good condition.
8. Today, ceramics are used to make some of the _____ of the space shuttle.
9. It's hard to believe that such _____ pictures were made by a young child.
10. Most cave paintings are of animals. _____, the paintings in Chauvet Cave show lions, horses, and even a panther.
11. The photos taken of the soccer match showed the players _____ .
12. Artists use _____ and color to add depth to their paintings.

C Vocabulary Review: Synonyms

Match the synonyms (words that mean the same).

_____ 1. durable	a. even
_____ 2. incredibly	b. disagreement
_____ 3. uniform	c. cure
_____ 4. extensive	d. indestructible
_____ 5. controversy	e. helper
_____ 6. heal	f. mostly
_____ 7. purpose	g. extraordinarily
_____ 8. assistant	h. first
_____ 9. original	i. reason
_____ 10. mainly	j. vast

d Comprehension Check: Multiple Choice

Circle the letter of the best answer.

1. Chauvet Cave was discovered _____.
   a. in the 19th century
   b. by Jean Clottes
   c. by amateurs

2. The paintings on the walls of Chauvet Cave are about _____ years old.
   a. 300
   b. 17,000
   c. 31,000

3. The paintings of animals in Chauvet Cave are _____.
   a. well preserved
   b. of one kind of animal
   c. very rough

4. The most sophisticated paintings in the cave are _____.
   a. very rough
   b. very realistic
   c. very stiff

5. Chauvet Cave is closed to tourists because _____.
   a. it's difficult to get to the cave
   b. visitors could damage the paintings
   c. it's located on privately owned land

6. The paintings in Chauvet Cave are well preserved because _____.
   a. they have been protected from light and air since they were made
   b. they were made with charcoal
   c. they are very sophisticated

7. The paintings in Chauvet Cave surprised archeologists because _____.
   a. they were so sophisticated
   b. they showed pictures of animals
   c. they were stiff and stylized

8. Before the discovery of Chauvet Cave, archeologists thought that_____.
   a. people painted for religious reasons
   b. exposing cave paintings to light and air wouldn't damage them
   c. people learned to draw and paint gradually over thousands of years

30

Comprehension Questions

1. How was Chauvet Cave discovered?
2. What is special about the paintings in Chauvet Cave?
3. What three words might you use to describe the best paintings in the cave?
4. What did the artists do to make the animal paintings look real?
5. According to the reading, there are three kinds of paintings in the cave. What are they?
6. Why are the paintings in the cave so well preserved?
7. Why is Chauvet Cave closed to the public?
8. How did the Chauvet Cave paintings change the way archeologists think about human development?

 Reading Strategy: Making Inferences

When you make an inference, you draw a logical conclusion based on the facts that you have.

Fact: Your friend has a broken arm.

Logical conclusion or inference: Your friend had an accident.

Illogical conclusion: Your friend fell down the stairs.

What can you infer from the information in each sentence below? Check (✓) the possible inferences.

1. When Eliette Deschamps noticed that there was a huge cave below the opening, the three explorers returned to their truck to get a ladder. Even though it was dark, they decided to go down into the cave.
   - ☐ They were eager to see what was in the cave.
   - ☐ It was unusual to find such a large cave.
   - ☐ The three explorers wanted to sleep in the cave.
   - ☐ The three explorers didn't usually go into caves at night.

2. When the French archeologist Jean Clottes was asked about the cave paintings, he said, "I was deeply moved when I saw the paintings. They're as good as any art made anywhere in the world."
   - ☐ Clottes liked the paintings.
   - ☐ Clottes was angry when he saw the paintings.
   - ☐ Clottes thought the paintings were very rough.
   - ☐ Clottes thinks the paintings are very sophisticated.

 31

g Vocabulary Expansion: Word Forms

Choose the right word form for each sentence below.

	Verb	Noun	Adjective	Adverb
1.	perfect	perfection imperfection	perfect imperfect	perfectly imperfectly
2.	mean	meaning	meaningful meaningless	
3.	trace	tracing		
4.		roughness	rough	roughly
5.		sophistication	sophisticated unsophisticated	
6.		amateur	amateur amateurish	
7.	identify	identification identity	identifiable	identifiably
8.	notice	notice	noticeable	noticeably

1. a. By the time she was three years old, she could write her name

   _____ .

   b. Athletes spend years trying to _____ their style.

2. a. Do you know the _____ of the word *stiff*?

   b. She said tomorrow, but I think she _____ to say the day after tomorrow.

3. If you put a clear piece of paper over the drawing, you can

   _____ it.

4. The _____ of some of the paintings surprised people.

5. The _____ of many ancient paintings shows that good art is nothing new.

6. He's usually a great actor, but last night he gave an _____ performance.

32

7. She _____ herself by giving her name and address.

8. The colors on the paintings were barely _____. I almost didn't _____ them.

h Grammar Review: Irregular Verbs

Study the irregular verbs in this list. Then choose the correct verb form to complete each sentence. Use a verb from line 1 in sentence 1, and so on.

	Present	Past	Past participle
1.	forgive	forgave	forgiven
2.	weave	wove	woven
3.	wind	wound	wound
4.	spread	spread	spread
5.	mean	meant	meant
6.	go	went	gone
7.	hold	held	held
8.	see	saw	seen

1. She never _____ her brother for leaving home.

2. He owns a tapestry _____ by the Navajo.

3. She _____ a bandage around her leg and then fastened it with tape.

4. International organizations are working to stop the _____ of serious diseases.

5. He _____ to call her yesterday, but he forgot.

6. How many times have you _____ to an art museum?

7. A big celebration was _____ soon after the discovery of the paintings.

8. Very few people have _____ the paintings in Chauvet Cave.

i Sentence Combining

Read the examples and the model combinations below. Then rewrite sentences 1 to 4 following the models.

Example: Some of the paintings are stiff and stylized. Others are quite rough.

Models: a. Some of the paintings are stiff and stylized, and others are quite rough.
  b. Some of the paintings are stiff and stylized, while others are quite rough.
  c. While some of the paintings are stiff and stylized, others are quite rough.

1. Some of the paintings show a type of lion. Other paintings are of horses.

  a. _____
  b. _____
  c. _____

2. One person pushed herself through the opening. The other two waited outside.

  a. _____
  b. _____
  c. _____

Example: Many caves in the world have been decorated with paintings. Chauvet Cave is one of them.

Models: a. One of many caves in the world that have been decorated with paintings is Chauvet Cave.
  b. Chauvet Cave is one of many caves in the world that have been decorated with paintings.
  c. Chauvet Cave, like many caves in the world, has been decorated with paintings.

3. Many archeologists have seen Chauvet Cave. Jean Clottes is one of them.

  a. _____
  b. _____
  c. _____

4. Many animals have become extinct. The wooly rhinoceros is one of them.

a. _____

b. _____

c. _____

j Writing

Imagine that you were the first person to see the paintings in Chauvet Cave. Write a short journal entry that tells what you saw and how you felt.

Graffiti

© Dana White/Photo Edit

Before You Read

1. What are the painters above using to paint the walls?

2. What is your opinion of the painting in the photo? Is it beautiful? Is it art?

3. Do you think people should be allowed to paint on public walls? Why or why not?

Context Clues

*The words in **bold** print below are from this lesson. Use context clues to guess what each word means.*

1. Many examples of graffiti are **carved** on the walls of the ancient city of Pompeii.

2. Some of the graffiti on walls in Pompeii are **declarations** of love, while others are insults.

3. Some of the graffiti in Pompeii are complaints about store owners who were **cheating** people.

4. Of course, not everyone likes or **approves** of graffiti on city walls.

5. The city of Los Angeles bought several "paint stores on wheels" to **combat** graffiti. These vans traveled around the city looking for graffiti and painting over them immediately.

4   Graffiti

A quiet street, a blank wall, a can of spray paint—and a young person goes to work writing graffiti. The term *graffiti* means words or drawings scratched or painted on a wall. The word comes from the Greek term
5   *graphein*, which means "to write." People have been writing graffiti on walls for thousands of years, but today some people believe that certain types of graffiti have **evolved** into a **genuine** art form.

developed; changed

true; real

Many of the oldest existing examples of graffiti are
10 from the ancient city of Pompeii on the western coast of Italy. In the year 79, Pompeii was destroyed by the eruption of Mt. Vesuvius. Ash from the volcano buried the city, preserving much of it for us to see today. **Carved** on the walls of Pompeii are many examples of graffiti.
15 Some of the graffiti are **declarations** of love, while others are insults. Some of the graffiti are complaints about store owners who were **cheating** people, while others are

political statements or rough drawings of people. Although the messages differ, the graffiti have one
20 important thing in common; they were all written without the permission of the owner of the wall. For historians, however, these graffiti are some of the few available sources of information about the lives of the common people of Pompeii and their everyday **concerns**.

25   While people have been writing graffiti on walls for thousands of years, in the 1960s a new type of graffiti started appearing on city walls in the United States. Some people called this type of graffiti "**gang** graffiti" because it was made by gang members to identify their **territory**. Gang graffiti consisted simply of the gang's
30 name, or "tag"; its purpose was to warn other gangs to stay away. A gang's tag had to be **<u>distinctive</u>** and easy to make quickly, but it was not meant to be artistic.

a group of young people who join together for support and protection

different from others; special

By the end of the 1970s, the practice of "tagging" was no longer mainly a gang activity. People who had
35 no connection to a gang were writing their names on flat surfaces all around the city. Their goal was to become famous by getting their name on as many surfaces as possible. However, as more and more people got involved in tagging, it became increasingly
40 difficult for writers to get attention. This led some writers to begin experimenting with ways to make their tags **<u>stand out</u>**. Some started making their tags bigger and **<u>bolder</u>,** while others combined letters with pictures. As tags became increasingly elaborate,
45 individual styles could be identified.

be noticeable; be easily seen

stronger; clearer

From tagging, graffiti developed into something called graffiti art, or aerosol art. Graffiti artists combined their unique letter styles with pictures to create large paintings that covered an entire wall or the
50 entire side of a subway car. During the 1970s and 1980s, the subway cars of New York became a moving museum of art for graffiti artists. The purpose of graffiti art, unlike that of gang graffiti, is self-expression and creativity. **According to** one graffiti artist, "Creating
55 graffiti is an art, and just like any other art, it requires tons of practice and work." Today, most graffiti art is

made with spray paint, although some artists also use brushes and markers. For graffiti artists, just about anything can serve as a surface for their artwork, even
60 rocks, roads, and billboards.

Of course not everyone likes or **approves** of the graffiti on city walls. In fact, most people think of creating graffiti as **vandalism** rather than art. For the majority of people, doing graffiti without someone's
65 permission is not freedom of expression; it is **arrogance**. And the **presence** of graffiti in their neighborhoods makes many people feel less safe. Seeing graffiti all around them makes many people feel that danger is just around the corner.

the destruction of property for fun

a feeling of self-importance

70 In the 1980s, many cities started taking action against graffiti. The city of New York, for example, started a **campaign** to **get rid of** graffiti on subway cars. By painting over the graffiti soon after they were made, the city was able to discourage graffiti artists from
75 decorating the subway cars. Then, in 1987, a new type of paint-resistant subway car became available, making it impossible for graffiti artists to paint on the cars. The city of Los Angeles bought several "paint stores on wheels" to **combat** graffiti. These vans traveled around
80 the city looking for graffiti and painting over them immediately. The city's goal was to discourage graffiti artists by painting over their graffiti within 24 hours. Other cities have used protective coatings and special building materials to prevent people from writing
85 graffiti. Although these solutions have been **effective**, they are very expensive.

an organized effort to do something

Does this mean the end of graffiti? Not quite. In some countries, such as Japan, England, and the United States, graffiti artists are allowed to do their work on
90 specially **designated** walls in a city. Graffiti art is shown in museums, and in Australia, well-known companies **sponsor** graffiti competitions. There are also hundreds of web sites dealing with graffiti art, as well as many books and instructional videos. And, of course, there are
95 still people who will try to leave their mark on someone else's wall.

chosen; specified

help to pay for

a   Vocabulary

evolve	carve	cheat	stand out
concern	approve	get rid of	sponsors
genuine	boldly	arrogant	according to

1. If you _____ on your taxes, you will get into trouble.

2. You can use a knife to _____ a piece of wood.

3. When you speak _____, people will stop to listen.

4. All cultures and languages _____ over time.

5. Do you have any old clothes that you want to _____?

6. Shirin's parents didn't _____ of her boyfriend because he was dishonest.

7. My boss is an _____ person. He really thinks he's more important than everyone else.

8. My neighbors painted their house pink so that it would

   _____.

9. Professional athletes sometimes wear the names of their

   _____ on their clothes.

10. The museum thought it owned a _____ Van Gogh painting, but in fact the painting was a copy.

11. _____ one theory, the presence of graffiti in an area makes people feel less safe.

12. Her parents expressed their _____ about her poor grades.

b Vocabulary

declared	concerned	gang	territory
distinctive	bold	vandalism	presence
campaign	combat	effective	designated

1. Many people feel nervous in the _____ of a famous person.
2. Would you join a _____ to stop children from smoking?
3. How _____ are you about the environment?
4. Soon after the two countries _____ war, they started fighting.
5. In most public places you can smoke only in specially _____ areas.
6. What is the most _____ way to get rid of a fever?
7. It costs a lot of money to _____ graffiti.
8. All famous fashion designers have a _____ style.
9. You can go to jail for _____.
10. Each salesperson in the company has a specific _____ to cover.
11. Young people sometimes join a _____ because they want to be part of a group.

c Vocabulary Review: Odd One Out

Circle the word that doesn't fit in each group.

1. adapt, cheat, evolve, change
2. get rid of, destroy, preserve, erase
3. genuine, extensive, vast, huge
4. approve of, agree with, preserve, like
5. indestructible, bold, durable, long-lasting
6. ancestors, artifacts, amateurs, sponsors
7. beautiful, distinctive, exquisite, attractive
8. kick, scratch, write, touch

d Comprehension Check: True/False/Not Enough Information

_____ 1. Ancient examples of graffiti still exist.

_____ 2. Ancient graffiti were painted on walls.

_____ 3. Modern graffiti are carved onto walls.

_____ 4. The purpose of gang graffiti is self-expression.

_____ 5. Graffiti artists started painting subway cars in New York in the 1950s.

_____ 6. The role of graffiti is a controversial topic.

_____ 7. The creation of graffiti is a form of vandalism.

_____ 8. Cities haven't spent much money removing graffiti.

_____ 9. Some cities provide special walls for graffiti artists to paint on.

_____10. There are fewer graffiti in New York today than there were 20 years ago.

e Comprehension Questions

1. Why did people in ancient Pompeii write graffiti on walls?
2. Why do historians find graffiti useful?
3. What is the purpose of gang graffiti?
4. What is a "tag"?
5. What do graffiti writers do to make their tags stand out?
6. How is a tag different from graffiti art?
7. How was ancient graffiti different from modern graffiti?
8. What is the future of graffiti?

Reading Strategy: Identifying the Main Idea

When you tell what a paragraph is about, you are identifying its topic. When you state the most important information about the topic, you are identifying its main idea.

In the chart below, identify the main idea in each paragraph of the reading on pages 37–39.

Paragraph	Topic	Main idea
1 (lines 1–8)	definition of graffiti	*Graffiti, or words and drawings written on walls, have been around for a long time.*
2 (lines 9–24)	ancient graffiti	*Graffiti provide us with information about people long ago.*
3 (lines 25–32)	gang graffiti	*A special kind of graffiti in the 1960s introduced gang graffiti.*
4 (lines 33–45)	tagging	
5 (lines 46–60)	graffiti art	
6 (lines 61–69)	attitudes toward graffiti	
7 (lines 70–86)	getting rid of graffiti	
8 (lines 87–96)	graffiti today	

43

g   Vocabulary Expansion: Collocations

Study the collocation chart below, and then complete the sentences.

get	attention approval rid of noticed broken

1. Sometimes children misbehave because they want to get their parents' _____.

2. If you dye your hair green, you will be sure to get _____.

3. If you want to get _____ a bad smell in the house, you can open the windows.

4. If you drop a piece of porcelain, it might get _____.

5. She couldn't get her parents' _____ to get married.

h   Grammar Review: Past Participles as Adjectives

The past participle form of a verb can be used as an adjective. The past participles of regular verbs end in *-ed*. They are the same as the past tense forms. Irregular verbs have irregular past participles.

Examples: a *painted* wall   a *discouraged* person
            a *destroyed* city   a *written* word

Choose one of the following past participles to complete each sentence below.

vandalized	required	carved	designated
woven	broken	concerned	baked

1. The museum owns several _____ tapestries made by the Navajo Indians.

2. English is a _____ course at this university.

3. We had _____ lasagna for dinner.

4. They tried to sell me a _____ toy.

5. There is a beautiful _____ design on the vase.

6. The _____ wall was quickly cleaned up by the city.

7. If there is a fire, you should go immediately to the _____ waiting area.

8. _____ parents should meet with their children's teachers to discuss the problem.

i | Sentence Combining

Read the example and the model combinations below. Then rewrite sentences 1 to 3 following the models.

Example: There are many examples of graffiti in Pompeii. They are carved on the walls.

Models: a. There are many examples of graffiti carved on the walls of Pompeii.
b. Many examples of graffiti are carved on the walls of Pompeii.
c. Carved on the walls of Pompeii are many examples of graffiti.

1. There are many kinds of graffiti. They are written or painted on walls.

    a. _____

    b. _____

    c. _____

2. There are vans that travel around the city. They are filled with cans of paint.

    a. _____

    b. _____

    c. _____

3. There are several international graffiti competitions. They are sponsored by famous companies.

    a. _____

    b. _____

    c. _____

j | Writing

Can graffiti be art? Write a paragraph in which you state your opinion and give reasons for it.

Video Highlights

a   Before You Watch

You are going to watch a video about the art of the Ndebele, one of South Africa's smallest ethnic groups. (See the photo.) Working in pairs, use the words below to describe Ndebele art:

modern	expert	beautiful	complicated
bold	extraordinary	traditional	skillful

© Roger De La Harpe; Gallo Images/CORBIS

b   As You Watch

1. First, look at the sentences below. Can you guess the missing word or words? Now watch the video and complete the sentences.

   a. In the beginning, the Ndebele built brown beehive-shaped huts. Today, Ndebele homes are _____.

   b. The artwork on the houses is done by _____.

c. People can't believe it, but when they paint the houses, the Ndebele work without _____.

d. There's a lot of competition, so each family has its own

_____.

e. The Ndebele are best known for the rings that the women wear around their _____.

2. Watch the video again. Write down the four types of art that are shown and a brief description of each.

Art	Description
photography	scenes from Ndebele life

Read the following quote from the video. Then answer the questions that follow as a group.

"Modern times have seen a decrease in the practice of cultural traditions. But the traditional Ndebele village is trying to preserve that artistic heritage."

1. Why are the Ndebele continuing their traditions?
2. How can art help to preserve culture?
3. Think about the lessons in this unit. How do these art forms reflect their cultures?
4. Are there any traditional villages in your country of origin? Describe them.
5. Would you like to live in a traditional village? Why or why not?

Crossword Puzzle

Across

2. the same on every side
9. The _____ of trained singers to the Navajo population of an area is very low.
11. A _____ item is much more valuable than a fake one.
12. unique
14. The ocean is too _____ for us to see where it ends.
15. not professional

Down

1. not smooth
3. thousands of years
4. the people who lived before us
5. objects left behind by ancient civilizations
6. Clay becomes hard when it is _____.
7. difficult to break
8. The Chauvet Cave paintings were _____ because they were not exposed to sunlight that could damage them.
10. unlike anything that came before
13. Gangs used "tags" to mark their _____.

Choosing the Correct Definition

Words often have more than one meaning. Read the dictionary definitions of *serve, mean,* and *concern.*

> **serve** /sɜrv/ *v.* **served, serving, serves 1** [I;T] to act or function as: *This table can serve as a desk.* **2** [I;T] to act as a servant, clerk, server, etc.: *The waitress served me coffee.* **3** [I;T] to be in public office: *The mayor served four years.* **4** [I;T] to put a ball into play: *to serve in tennis* **5** [T] (in law) to give officially: *A sheriff served a summons on the woman to appear in court.*
>
> **mean** /min/ *v.* **meant** /mɛnt/, **meaning** /'miniŋ/, **means 1** [T] to indicate, have significance: *That flashing red light means to stop your car and wait for the train to go by.* | | *What does this word mean?* **2** [T] to intend to, want to do s.t.: *I meant to call home, but forgot to do it.*
> *-adj.* **1** wanting to hurt s.o.: *That boy is mean, a real bully.* **2** *frml.* extremely bad in quality: *During dry periods, poor farmers can lead a mean existence.*
>
> **con-cern** /kən'sɜrn/ *n.* **1** [C;U] care, attention: *He shows constant concern about how his mother is feeling.*
> *-v.* [T] **1** to be about: *This letter concerns payment for my new TV.* **2** to deal with, care about, or worry about: *His mother's sickness concerns him a great deal.*

Now read the sentences on the next page. Fill in each blank with the correct form of the correct word (*serve, mean,* or *concern*). Tell what part of speech the word is and write the number of the appropriate definition next to each sentence.

	Part of speech	Definition number
1. His mother's sickness _concerns_ him a great deal.	_verb_	_2_
2. The waitress _____ me coffee.		
3. That boy is _____, a real bully.		
4. The mayor _____ four years.		
5. This letter _____ payment for my new TV.		
6. During dry periods, poor farmers can lead a _____ existence.		
7. I _____ to call home, but forgot to do it.		
8. This table can _____ as a desk.		
9. What does this word _____?		
10. He shows constant _____ about how his mother is feeling.		
11. The tennis player _____ the ball to her opponent.		

Organizations

unit

2

An isolated individual does not exist.
He who is sad, saddens others.
—Antoine de Saint-Exupéry

© 2002 Landov LLC

The United Nations

lesson

1

© 2002 Landov LLC

Before You Read

1. What do you already know about the United Nations?

2. Why was the United Nations recently in the news?

3. Do you think the United Nations is an effective organization? Why or why not?

Context Clues

*The words in **bold** print below are from this lesson. Use context clues to guess what each word means.*

1. The **charter** of the United Nations (UN) lists the four main goals and purposes of the organization.

2. The **headquarters** of the United Nations is in New York City. This is where the General Assembly of the United Nations meets every year.

3. Five members of the UN Security Council are permanent members. The remaining 10 members are **elected** by the General Assembly.

4. The United Nations also organizes large international meetings, where people meet to discuss important world **issues**. One meeting was about the uses and ownership of oceans.

1   The United Nations

In 1945, **delegates** from 50 countries met in San Francisco, California, to make plans for an organization called the United Nations. World War II had just ended, millions of people had died, and there was destruction
5 everywhere. People hoped they could build a future of world peace through this new organization.

The **charter** of the United Nations (UN) <u>states</u> the four main goals and purposes of the organization. They are

says formally

10 1. To work together for international peace and to solve international problems;
2. To develop friendly relations among nations;
3. To work together for human rights for everyone of all races, religions, languages, and of both sexes; and
15 4. To build a center where nations can work together for these goals.

The United Nations has grown from an organization of 51 countries in 1945 to 191 nations in 2004. Today, almost every country in the world is a member of the
20 UN. Each country that joins the United Nations signs an agreement that says:

1. All members are equal.
2. All members promise to solve international problems in a peaceful way.
25 3. No member will use force against another member.
4. All members will help the UN in its actions.
5. The UN will not try to solve problems within countries except to enforce international peace.

The **headquarters** of the United Nations is in New
30 York City. This is where the General Assembly, the main body of the United Nations, meets every year from September to December. The General Assembly is made up of **representatives** from each member country, who discuss issues related to peace and security and make
35 recommendations. However, the General Assembly

54

does not have the power to enforce its recommendations. A second UN body, the 15-member Security Council, has the main **responsibility** for **maintaining** international peace. Five members—

> duty

40 Britain, China, France, the Russian Federation, and the United States—are permanent members of the Security Council. The remaining 10 members are **elected** by the General Assembly and serve two-year terms. A third organ of the UN, the **Economic** and Social Council, is

> related to the study of how society uses resources

45 responsible for the social and economic work of the UN.

Over the years, the United Nations has had some **successes** in its **role** of world peacemaker. It has **negotiated** 172 peaceful **settlements** and helped to end two wars. It has also helped to slow the spread of

> achievements; good results
>
> job; position
>
> brought people together to talk about and agree on

50 nuclear weapons by inspecting nuclear **facilities** in 90 countries.

As a peacekeeper, the UN has also had a number of successes. Since 1945, UN peacekeeping forces have been involved in 56 **missions**. They have supervised

55 **ceasefires** and the **withdrawal** of **troops,** and they have monitored elections. Over the years, roughly 130 nations have participated in the peacekeeping missions. In 1988, the UN peacekeeping forces received the Nobel Peace Prize. Unfortunately, member nations have been

> groups of soldiers

60 unwilling to give UN peacekeeping forces the independence and financial support they need to be even more effective.

In **evaluating** the success of the UN, it is important to keep in mind that the organization has many

> making a judgment about

65 functions in addition to preventing or ending wars. The United Nations is really a "family" of related organizations, which are working to provide a better life for people everywhere. One part of the UN family is UNICEF, an organization that provides food, medical

70 care, and many other services to poor children wherever they live. Thanks to the efforts of UNICEF, the immunization rate of children in developing countries has jumped from 5 percent in 1974 to more than 80 percent today. Another part of the UN family is the

75 World Health Organization (WHO), which develops medical programs for people all over the world. In 1980,

WHO **announced** that, after 13 years of work, it had succeeded in ridding the world of the disease smallpox.

80 To support its humanitarian efforts, the UN employs thousands of people all around the world. They work as planners to increase production in farming and industry. They provide medical services, improve education programs, and spread scientific information. They develop programs that provide jobs and better

85 living conditions. They also help countries control their population growth.

The United Nations also organizes large international **conferences**, where people meet to discuss important world **issues**. One conference was about the

90 uses and ownership of oceans; another was about women. The United Nations also designates a **specific** problem for people to **focus on** each year. For example, the year 2003 was declared the International Year of Fresh Water. During these special years, people work

95 together to find solutions to the designated problems.

Many people believe that the best way for the United Nations to work for world peace is through its humanitarian activities. They hope that promoting contact and communication among people will make

100 wars less likely.

professional meetings

a   Vocabulary

delegates	charter	state	headquarters
responsibility	facilities	conferences	negotiate
election	maintain	announced	specific

1. It's the job of the landlord to _____ the apartment building in good condition.

2. The _____ of the company is in an expensive new building.

3. Many professions have annual _____ so that people can meet and share ideas.

4. We chose five _____ to go to the meeting and then report back to us.

5. Some think it's the mother's _____ to discipline the children, while others say it's the father's duty.

6. It took months to write the _____ of the United Nations.

7. The price of the car is $5,000, and the owner won't _____.

8. Just _____ your name and address. Don't say anything else.

9. We were surprised when the owner of the store _____ that he was moving away.

10. The sports _____ at my university are great. There is a swimming pool, a skating rink, and several soccer fields.

11. She didn't have a _____ reason for quitting the job. She just wasn't very happy there.

12. Half of the people in town voted on _____ day.

b Vocabulary

focus on	representatives	roles	economic
success	settlement	mission	ceasefire
troops	withdrew	evaluate	issues

1. One of the UN's _____ is to supervise nuclear facilities.

2. He _____ his hand quickly from the box when he saw a snake sitting in the bottom.

3. It takes luck and hard work to be a _____.

4. In their divorce _____, the husband and wife divided their money equally.

5. The school's _____ is to educate children to be curious and open-minded.

6. It's difficult to _____ your work when there is a lot of noise in the room.

7. In order to give you a grade, your teacher must _____ your work.

8. During the conflict, the _____ kept the people in the town safe.

9. A _____ was called after the warring sides agreed to peace talks.

10. One of the most serious _____ problems in the country is the shortage of jobs.

11. Each state sends two _____ to the U.S. Senate.

12. This year, the organization will be focusing on the _____ of air and water pollution.

c Vocabulary Review: Antonyms

Match the antonyms (words that are opposite in meaning).

_____	1. evil	a.	fragile
_____	2. properly	b.	uneven
_____	3. durable	c.	hide
_____	4. entire	d.	give in
_____	5. uniform	e.	incorrectly
_____	6. resist	f.	useless
_____	7. expose	g.	good
_____	8. effective	h.	part

d Comprehension Check: True/False/Not Enough Information

_____ 1. The United Nations was organized at the beginning of World War II.

_____ 2. The General Assembly has more members than the Security Council.

_____ 3. The members of the Security Council never change.

_____ 4. The UN has the responsibility for closing nuclear facilities in different countries.

_____ 5. The UN peacekeeping forces are responsible for holding elections in different countries.

_____ 6. The UN is involved in many humanitarian activities.

_____ 7. Every year, the UN has a special conference that focuses on water problems.

_____ 8. The number of UN member countries has increased since 1945.

_____ 9. Kuwait is a member of the UN.

_____ 10. The United Nations helped Algeria become independent.

 e Comprehension Questions

1. What is one of the UN's humanitarian activities?
2. What are three of the main organizations of the United Nations?
3. What is the difference between the General Assembly and the Security Council?
4. What is the role of the UN peacekeeping forces?
5. What does the UN do to end wars?
6. What role has the UN played in the fight against smallpox?
7. How has the UN been successful?
8. How has the UN been unsuccessful?
9. Why are there wars even though UN members agree not to fight?
10. What do you think people talked about at the UN conference on oceans?

f Reading Strategy: Identifying Main Ideas and Details

In the chart below, identify the main idea in each paragraph. Then summarize the most important details in your own words.

Paragraph	Main idea	Details
1 (lines 1–6)	People met in 1945 to set up the United Nations.	They were from 50 countries. They wanted to set up an organization that would bring peace to the world.
2 (lines 7–16)		
3 (lines 17–28)		
4 (lines 29–45)		
5 (lines 46–51)		
6 (lines 52–62)		
7 (lines 63–78)		
8 (lines 79–86)		
9 (lines 87–95)		

e Vocabulary Expansion: Word Forms

Choose the right word form for each sentence below.

	Verb	Noun	Adjective	Adverb
1.	delegate	delegate delegation		
2.	state	statement		
3.	maintain	maintenance		
4.		responsibility	responsible	responsibly
5.	represent	representative representation		
6.	announce	announcer announcement		
7.	succeed	success	successful	successfully
8.	supervise	supervisor supervision	supervisory	
9.	negotiate	negotiator negotiation		
10.	withdraw	withdrawal		

1. The government sent a _____ of experts to the meeting.
2. The president made a short _____ at the end of the meeting.
3. He studies hard to _____ his good grades.
4. His parents will let him use their car as long as he drives _____ .
5. My boss couldn't go to the conference, so I had to _____ her.
6. They _____ the results of the election 12 hours after it ended.
7. The UN hasn't always been _____ in preventing wars.
8. The _____ of the project was responsible for all the problems.

60

9. The peace _____ lasted for several years.

10. The troops refused to _____.

 ## h Grammar Review: Noun Substitutes

In English, we often use a pronoun to replace a noun or noun phrase that has already been used in the sentence or in a previous sentence.

Example: The (UN) has had some success in its role of world peacemaker. **It** has negotiated 172 peaceful settlements and helped to end two wars.

*Read the following sentences. Each pronoun is in **bold** print. Circle the noun or noun phrase that it replaces.*

1. The peacekeeping forces have been involved in 56 missions. **They** have supervised ceasefires and monitored elections.

2. UNICEF provides help to children wherever **they** live.

3. In 1980, WHO announced that, after 13 years of work, **it** had succeeded in ridding the world of smallpox.

4. To support **its** humanitarian efforts, the UN employs thousands of people.

5. The UN employs thousands of people. **They** provide medical services and spread scientific information.

6. One conference took place in the 1970s. **It** was about the uses of oceans.

7. Although the UN has had some successes, **it** has not been able to stop all wars.

8. The charter of the UN states the goals of the organization, but **it** does not say how the UN will meet these goals.

i Sentence Combining

Read the example and the different model combinations below. Then rewrite sentences 1 and 2 following the models.

Example: The General Assembly is made up of representatives from member countries. They discuss important issues related to peace.

Models: a. The General Assembly is made up of representatives from member countries who discuss important issues related to peace.
  b. The General Assembly, which is made up of representatives from member countries, discusses important issues related to peace.
  c. Representatives of member countries who make up the General Assembly discuss important issues related to peace.

1. The Security Council has representatives from 15 countries. They have the main responsibility for maintaining peace.

  a. _____
  b. _____
  c. _____

2. The UN peacekeeping forces are made up of people from many different countries. They monitor elections and supervise ceasefires.

  a. _____
  b. _____
  c. _____

j Writing

Do you have any ideas about how people in the world could live together more peacefully? Write about your ideas.

lesson 2

Amnesty International

© 2002 Landov LLC

Before You Read

1. What do you know about the organization Amnesty International?

2. Why are the people in the picture protesting?

3. Can you think of anyone who was imprisoned for his or her political or religious beliefs?

Context Clues

*The words in **bold** print below are from this lesson. Use context clues to guess what each word means.*

1. In 1960, two students in Portugal were put jail for seven years. The reason? They had made critical **remarks** about their government. In England, a lawyer by the name of Peter Benenson read about this **incident** and decided he had to do something.

2. To maintain its **impartiality**, Amnesty International is careful to remain independent of all national governments.

3. In 1977, Amnesty International was **awarded** the Nobel Peace Prize.

4. In the 1980s, Amnesty International was able to increase the size of its **staff** and the number of offices worldwide.

2   Amnesty International

In 1960, two students in Portugal were **sentenced** to seven years in **prison**. The reason? They had made critical **remarks** about their government. In England, a lawyer by the name of Peter Benenson read about this
5 **incident** and decided he had to do something. Benenson wrote a newspaper article called "The Forgotten Prisoners." In it, he told about six people in six different countries who were in prison because of their beliefs. In the newspaper article, Benenson asked
10 readers to join him in a year-long campaign against the imprisonment of people for their political or religious beliefs. It was Benenson's hope that people would write letters to government officials calling for the **release** of these prisoners. In the first months of the campaign,
15 people sent thousands of letters demanding the release of the prisoners. By the end of 1961, the campaign had developed into a permanent international organization called Amnesty International, and it was already working on the **cases** of 210 prisoners.
20   Amnesty International's primary goal is to obtain the release of "prisoners of **conscience**." These are people who have been imprisoned for their beliefs; they have neither used violence themselves nor encouraged anyone else to use violence. Toni Ambatielos, one of the
25 six prisoners of conscience whom Benenson wrote about in 1961, was put in prison for his trade union activities. Another one of the prisoners, Dr. Agostino Neto, was jailed for trying to improve health care in his country.
30   In the 1960s, many Amnesty members formed small groups to "adopt" a prisoner of conscience. When a group adopted a prisoner of conscience, it concentrated on helping that specific prisoner. Members of the group would regularly write letters to officials in the

given as a punishment

event; happening

    65

35 prisoner's government, and when possible, they would try to help the prisoner's family. Today, there are more than 2,000 adoption groups, each focusing its efforts on two or more prisoners.

As Amnesty International grew, it expanded its
40 mission to include other victims of human rights **abuse**. Today, the organization is working to make sure all prisoners get a **fair trial** and to end all types of **torture**. It is also involved in a major campaign to end the death **penalty**.

abuse — cruel treatment

torture — extreme physical abuse

penalty — punishment

45 Amnesty International has become an effective organization in large part because of its **impartiality** and **reliability**. To maintain its impartiality, Amnesty is careful to remain independent of all national governments. It gets its money from individual
50 **contributions** and special events. To maintain its reliability, Amnesty puts much time, effort, and money into getting **accurate** information about prisoners. Research teams carefully check the facts about human rights abuses. Fact-finding teams interview prisoners,
55 family members, **witnesses**, and government officials. This information is used to create a **profile** with the facts about each person's imprisonment.

contributions — gifts of money

witnesses — people who saw something happen and can tell about it

Amnesty International works to help individual prisoners; it does not try to change the governments
60 that are holding the prisoners of conscience. After some negative **publicity** in the late 1960s, Amnesty International adopted a rule that members of the organization could not work on cases inside their own country. The organization worried that members
65 working in their own country would not be able to stay impartial.

publicity — information in the media that creates public interest in something

In 1977, Amnesty International was **awarded** the Nobel Peace Prize. In the same year, Steve Biko, an African anti-apartheid activist, was imprisoned for his
70 political activities. While Biko was in prison, he was tortured and eventually **murdered** for his beliefs. A popular musician named Peter Gabriel wrote a song called "Biko" to protest his murder and to support the work of Amnesty International. Over 25 years later,

66

75 when audiences hear the song "Biko," they often stand
and join in the singing. In the mid-1980s, Amnesty
International was helped by a number of other well-
known musicians. To help the organization, the
musicians gave concerts and contributed their profits to
80 Amnesty International. The concerts gave the
organization **valuable** publicity as well as financial
support, and it was able to increase the size of its <u>staff</u>   employees
and the number of offices worldwide. In 2004, the
United States chapter of Amnesty International released
85 the *Music for Human Rights* CD with some of the hottest
musicians of the year and offered it for free to new
members. The support of popular musicians helped to
inform young people and interest them in Amnesty
International.
90   Amnesty International now has 1.5 million members
in 162 countries. It continues to petition for
improvements in prisons, the end of torture, and the
release of prisoners of conscience. Amnesty members
continue to tirelessly write letters and hold benefits,
95 vigils, and fundraisers for prisoners of conscience
around the world. And what happened to the six
prisoners of conscience whom Benenson wrote about in
1961? All of them eventually gained their freedom.

a Vocabulary

sentenced	prison	remarks	incidents
release	cases	conscience	staff
torture	fair	trial	penalty

1. Not being allowed to sleep is one of the worst forms
   of _____.

2. Another word for *jail* is _____.

3. The teacher discovered several _____ of cheating on the
   final exam.

4. What is a _____ punishment for cheating on a test?

67

5. He was _____ to 10 years in prison for cheating the company of thousands of dollars.

6. During the murder _____, several witnesses told what they had seen.

7. When you _____ a balloon or a kite, it usually goes up in the air.

8. There have been two _____ in which people have been caught stealing from our office.

9. More than 500 people are part of the organization's _____.

10. No one in the class made any _____ about the difficulty of the exam.

11. What is the _____ for paying your taxes late?

12. His _____ is bothering him because he lied to his friends and family.

b Vocabulary

impartial	reliable	contributions	accurate
witness	profile	publicity	award
murder	valuable	staff	abuse

1. I don't take my car on long trips because it isn't very _____.

2. Most people would probably say that gold is more _____ than silver.

3. Movie companies spend a lot of money on _____ for their films.

4. It's difficult for parents to be _____ when they are talking about their own children.

5. Everyone who is a member of the company's _____ is invited to the party.

6. The punishment for _____ is harsh.

7. Have you ever gotten an _____ for something?

8. If you _____ a car accident, you should report what you saw.

9. It's possible to _____ someone mentally or physically.

10. The newspaper did a wonderful _____ of the town, giving its history and politics.

11. Thousands of people made _____ to help the victims of the flood.

12. Everything in the report was _____ except the date.

C Vocabulary Review: Definitions

Match the words with their definitions.

_____ 1. negotiate   a. be noticeable

_____ 2. withdraw   b. bake at a high temperature

_____ 3. stand out   c. make last for a long time

_____ 4. possess   d. take back

_____ 5. fire   e. destroy

_____ 6. preserve   f. copy

_____ 7. combat   g. discuss in order to come to an agreement

_____ 8. vandalize   h. spread

                              i. fight

                              j. own

d Comprehension Check: Multiple Choice

Circle the letter of the best answer.

1. Peter Benenson was a _____ in England.
   a. newspaper reporter
   b. lawyer
   c. student

2. Benenson wanted to help _____.
   a. prisoners of conscience
   b. forgotten prisoners
   c. all prisoners

3. Dr. Agostino Neto is an example of a _____.
   a. member of Amnesty International
   b. prisoner of conscience
   c. trade union member

4. Amnesty International is against _____.
   a. fair trials
   b. impartiality
   c. the death penalty

5. Amnesty International spends a lot of time and money to _____.
   a. get accurate information about prisoners
   b. attract new members to the organization
   c. fight against negative publicity

6. Members of Amnesty International cannot work on cases _____.
   a. with other members
   b. that get a lot of publicity
   c. inside their own country

7. Staying independent of all national governments helps Amnesty International to be _____.
   a. impartial
   b. flexible
   c. focused

8. Amnesty International has been around since _____.
   a. 1977
   b. 1969
   c. 1961

e   Comprehension Questions

1. How did Amnesty International get started?
2. What inspired Peter Benenson to start Amnesty International?
3. Why does letter writing sometimes work to get the release of a prisoner?
4. What is a prisoner of conscience?
5. What do Toni Ambatielos and Dr. Neto have in common?
6. How does Amnesty International stay impartial?
7. Why is Amnesty International thought to be a reliable organization?
8. Why can't members work on cases in their own countries?
9. Who was Steve Biko?
10. How did Peter Gabriel help Amnesty International?

f Reading Strategy: Taking Notes in a Chart

Before you write a summary of a reading, it can help to make a chart of categories of information.

Complete the chart below with information about Amnesty International.

AMNESTY INTERNATIONAL

Goals	Actions/activities	Successes

g Vocabulary Expansion: Prefixes

The prefixes *un-*, *im-*, *dis-*, *in-*, and *non-* can be put at the beginning of some words to add the meaning "not" to the word.

Choose the correct word from the pair to complete the sentence.

1. partial, impartial
2. reliable, unreliable
3. accurate, inaccurate
4. successful, unsuccessful
5. supervised, unsupervised

6. fairly, unfairly
7. effective, ineffective
8. concerned, unconcerned
9. approved, disapproved
10. original, unoriginal

1. I like all types of ice cream, but I'm really _____ to chocolate.

2. He lost his job because he was so _____.

3. The date on the message is _____. It should say June 12, not June 10.

4. I think she has been _____ because she doesn't try very hard.

5. Young children shouldn't be left at home _____.

6. They won the game _____; no one cheated.

7. If the medicine is _____, you'll get better soon.

8. I don't understand why they are so _____ about the air pollution in their area.

9. They _____ of the government's action, but there was nothing they could do about it.

10. She wrote a very _____ story. I've never read anything like it.

h Grammar Review: Prepositions

Write the missing prepositions on the lines.

In 1960, two students (1) _____ Portugal were sentenced to seven years (2) _____ prison. The reason? They had made critical remarks (3) _____ their government. In England, a lawyer by the name of Peter Benenson read (4) _____ this incident and decided he had to do something. Benenson wrote a newspaper article called "The Forgotten Prisoners." In it, he told about six people (5) _____ six different countries who were (6) _____ prison because (7) _____ their beliefs. In the newspaper article, Benenson asked readers to join him (8) _____ a year-long campaign (9) _____ the imprisonment of people (10) _____ their political or religious beliefs. It was Benenson's hope that people would write letters to government officials calling for the release (11) _____ these prisoners. In the first months of the campaign, people sent thousands of letters demanding the release (12) _____ the prisoners. By the end (13) _____ 1961, the campaign had developed (14) _____ a permanent international organization called Amnesty International, and it was already working on the cases (15) _____ 210 prisoners.

i   Sentence Combining

Read the example and the model combinations below. Then rewrite sentences 1 and 2 following the models.

Example: Amnesty International wants to maintain its impartiality. To do this, it remains independent of all governments.

Models: a. To remain impartial, Amnesty International remains independent of all governments.
             b. Amnesty International maintains its impartiality by remaining independent of all governments.
             c. Amnesty International remains independent of all governments in order to maintain its impartiality.

1. Amnesty International wants to maintain its reliability. To do this, it spends a lot of time and money getting accurate information.

   a. _____

   b. _____

   c. _____

2. Amnesty International wants to gain the release of prisoners of conscience. To do this, it starts letter-writing campaigns.

   a. _____

   b. _____

   c. _____

j   Writing

Have you ever written a letter because you wanted to change something? Write a letter to the director of your school about something you would like to change about your school. When you finish, share your letter with a classmate.

lesson

3

UNICEF

© SHEHZAD NOORANI/Peter Arnold, Inc.

Before You Read

1. What do you know about UNICEF?

2. How does UNICEF help children?

3. What kinds of help do you think children in the world need?

Context Clues

*The words in **bold** print below are from this lesson. Use context clues to guess what each word means.*

1. The **acronym** UNICEF means United Nations International Children's Emergency Fund.

2. UNICEF was created by the United Nations in 1946 to provide temporary help to children. In 1950, UNICEF's responsibilities were **expanded** to providing long-term help to children and mothers in all developing countries.

3. Among UNICEF's successes are the **eradication** of smallpox and the near eradication of polio.

4. **Globally**, there are now 42 million people with HIV/AIDS.

5. In cases of natural **disasters**, such as floods and earthquakes, UNICEF is able to respond quickly to people's needs, especially the needs of children.

3   UNICEF

The **acronym** UNICEF **stands for** United Nations International Children's **Emergency** Fund. This organization was created by the United Nations in 1946 to provide emergency help to children in post-war
5 Europe and China. In 1950, UNICEF's responsibilities were **expanded** to providing long-term help to children and mothers in all developing countries. Three years later, UNICEF became a permanent part of the United Nations system, and its name was changed to United
10 Nations Children's Fund. Despite the name change, the acronym UNICEF was kept, and today most people know of the organization by its acronym rather than its name.

UNICEF works with the governments of individual
15 countries to provide three kinds of services. It plans and develops programs, trains people to work in these programs, and provides the supplies and equipment to help the programs function. The programs that UNICEF develops cover five main areas: immunization,
20 education for girls, child protection, early childhood development, and HIV/AIDS.

In the area of immunization, UNICEF has had many successes, but it still has much work to do. Among its successes are the **eradication** of smallpox, the near
25 eradication of polio, and a <u>sharp</u> decrease in the   **sudden**
numbers of deaths from measles and tetanus. However, there are still countries that do not provide **routine** immunization, and in these countries diseases such as measles, diphtheria, whooping cough, tuberculosis, and
30 tetanus **persist**. According to UNICEF, more than 2 million children die each year from diseases that could have been prevented by inexpensive vaccines.

A second goal of UNICEF is giving children the best possible start in life. In fact, more than half of UNICEF's
35 <u>budget</u> is used to help children in their first years of life   **a plan to spend**
by providing them with better health care, nutrition,   **money or resources**

water, sanitation, and education. But the needs of young children around the world are **overwhelming**.

upsetting; overpowering

According to UNICEF, "out of 100 children born in a
40 year, 30 will most likely suffer from **malnutrition** in their first five years of life, 26 will not be immunized against the basic childhood diseases, 19 will lack **access**

the ability to get

to safe drinking water and 40 to **adequate** sanitation,

not bad, but not very good; minimal

and 17 will never go to school." Each year, these
45 problems cause the death of 11 million children under the age of 5. That means each day 30,000 children die, and most of these deaths could be prevented.

One of the biggest challenges facing UNICEF today is HIV/AIDS. **Globally**, there are now 42 million people
50 with HIV/AIDS; more than 3 million of them are children under the age of 15, and 12 million are young people between the ages of 15 and 24. One of the primary reasons for the increase in the number of HIV/AIDS cases is **ignorance** about how the disease is
55 spread. **Surveys** done in 60 countries have revealed that the majority of young people do not understand how HIV/AIDS is **transmitted** from one person to another. To change this, UNICEF focuses much of its attention on educating young people about the disease. In
60 addition to its educational programs, UNICEF is also involved in taking care of people with the disease and protecting them from **discrimination**.

While much of UNICEF's work is now in long-term projects, it still plays a **vital** role in emergency

very important

65 situations. In cases of natural **disasters**, such as floods and earthquakes, UNICEF is able to respond quickly to people's needs, especially the needs of children. For example, when monsoon rains caused rivers in Bangladesh to flood in 2004, millions of people were
70 affected. The floods **contaminated** drinking water

made unsafe or dirty

supplies, quickly spreading disease. UNICEF was able to move in quickly with medical supplies and equipment to set up sanitation systems. The organization's rapid response to disaster prevented the
75 deaths of many children. Again, when a tsunami hit countries in southeast Asia in 2004, UNICEF was able to

rush relief assistance to the area to help the survivors. In
addition to providing safe drinking water in order to
prevent the spread of disease, UNICEF was involved in
80 helping thousands of children who were separated from
or lost their parents when the tsunami hit, as well as
many more who were **traumatized** by the event.

shocked
emotionally

How does UNICEF pay for all this? Three-fourths of
the organization's money comes from the contributions
85 of governments. The remaining one-fourth comes from
individual contributions, the sale of UNICEF's greeting
cards and products, and special events held to collect
money for the organization. For example, in 2004, a chef
in London decided he had to do something to help the
90 victims of the tsunami. He organized an event called
UNICHEF, in which more than 150 restaurants joined
together to raise money for UNICEF's Tsunami
Children's Emergency Appeal. Restaurants
participating in the UNICHEF event **donated** a large
95 part of their earnings. With the help of people and
organizations like that, UNICEF will be able to continue
helping children around the world.

a Vocabulary

acronym	stand for	emergency	expands
eradicate	sharp	routine	global
budget	overwhelming	malnutrition	access

1. Do you know what the stars on the U.S. flag _____?

2. What number would you call in an _____?

3. The expression UNESCO is an _____ for United Nations
   Economic and Social Council.

4. If you feel a _____ pain in your chest, you should probably
   go to the hospital right away.

5. If UNICEF can _____ polio, no one will ever get the
   disease again.

6. The number of stars in the sky is _____. I can't believe how many there are.

7. Only a few people have _____ to the president's office.

8. Most individuals and companies have a _____ so that they won't spend more than they earn.

9. When a company or business _____, it has to increase the size of its staff.

10. When an activity becomes _____, you don't think about it anymore. You just do it.

11. _____ is a problem wherever people lack healthy food.

b Vocabulary

adequate	global	ignorant	surveyed
transmit	discriminate	vital	disaster
contaminated	traumatize	donated	persistent

1. It's against the law to _____ against someone because of his or her race, religion, age, or gender.

2. If you drink _____ water, you can get very sick.

3. Watching something terrible happen can _____ a child.

4. Access to clean water is _____.

5. Many children do not have access to _____ sanitation.

6. Soon after the earthquake, another _____ hit the area.

7. To find out what young people are interested in, we _____ more than 500 people.

8. You can _____ an e-mail message from the United States to China in seconds.

9. HIV/AIDS is a _____ problem.

10. A _____ person keeps trying. He or she doesn't give up easily.

11. Many people _____ food and clothes to help the victims of the fire.

12. If you can't get access to the facts, you will remain _____.

C Vocabulary Review: Synonyms

Match the synonyms.

_____ 1. torture   a. dependable

_____ 2. remarked   b. representative

_____ 3. reliable   c. primarily

_____ 4. mainly   d. donate

_____ 5. delegate   e. abuse

_____ 6. immunization   f. bold

_____ 7. impartial   g. fair

_____ 8. contribute   h. incident

                                     i. vaccination

                                     j. said

d Comprehension Check: Multiple Choice

Circle the letter of the best answer.

1. UNICEF became a permanent part of the UN system in _____.
   a. 1946
   b. 1950
   c. 1953

2. UNICEF has always been a _____ organization.
   a. temporary
   b. permanent
   c. UN

3. UNICEF does *not* focus on _____.
   a. disease prevention
   b. peace negotiations
   c. immunization

4. UNICEF is still working to eradicate _____.
   a. measles
   b. smallpox
   c. vaccinations

5. When drinking water gets _____, disease can spread quickly.
   a. traumatized
   b. contaminated
   c. transmitted

6. More children lack _____ than access to safe drinking water.
   a. adequate sanitation
   b. adequate education
   c. adequate health care

7. More than 3 million children under the age of 15 have _____.
   a. smallpox
   b. measles
   c. HIV/AIDS

8. To stop the spread of HIV/AIDS among young people, UNICEF needs to provide _____.
   a. education about the disease
   b. safe drinking water
   c. routine immunization

e Comprehension Questions

1. How has UNICEF changed over the years?
2. What three services does UNICEF provide to the governments of individual countries?
3. What are UNICEF's five main programs?
4. How has UNICEF been successful in the area of immunization?
5. In which area does UNICEF spend the largest part of its budget?
6. What are the goals of UNICEF's early childhood programs?
7. How many children are there with HIV/AIDS?
8. Why are people with HIV/AIDS discriminated against?
9. What are three kinds of disasters?
10. What can individuals do to help UNICEF in its work for children?

Reading Strategy: Using a Dictionary

Use a dictionary to find the definition of each acronym below.

1. NATO _____
2. NAFTA _____
3. UN _____

 Vocabulary Expansion: Word Forms

Choose the right word form for each sentence below.

	Verb	Noun	Adjective	Adverb
1.	expand	expanse expansion	expansive	expansively
2.	eradicate	eradication		
3.	persist	persistence	persistent	persistently
4.	transmit	transmission		
5.	discriminate	discrimination	discriminatory	
6.	contaminate	contamination		
7.	traumatize	trauma	traumatic	traumatically
8.	donate	donation		
9.	ignore	ignorance	ignorant	ignorantly
10.	access	access	accessible	

1. They _____ their house by adding a third floor.
2. It's difficult to _____ certain kinds of weeds.
3. If you are _____, you will eventually get a job.
4. The _____ of radio signals was interrupted by the bad weather.
5. In the 1950s, many laws were _____.

6. _____ of drinking water can cause the death of thousands of people.

7. The destruction of the town was a _____ event for everyone.

8. Some people _____ money to Amnesty International, while others give their time.

9. If you are _____ of something, you can't change it.

10. Today, public buildings must be _____ to people in wheelchairs.

h Grammar Review: Articles

Write an article in each blank if one is needed.

(1) _____ acronym UNICEF stands for (2) _____ United Nations International Children's Emergency Fund. This organization was created by (3) _____ United Nations in 1946 to provide emergency help to children in post-war (4) _____ Europe and China. In 1950, (5) _____ UNICEF's responsibilities were expanded to providing long-term help to (6) _____ children and mothers in all developing countries. Three years later, UNICEF became (7) _____ permanent part of (8) _____ United Nations system, and its name was changed to (9) _____ United Nations Children's Fund. Despite (10) _____ name change, (11) _____ acronym UNICEF was kept, and today most people know of (12) _____ organization by its acronym rather than its name.

i Sentence Combining

Read the example and the model combinations below. Then rewrite sentences 1 and 2 following the models.

Example: UNICEF has had many successes. However, it still has much work to do.

Models: a. Although UNICEF has had many successes, it still has much work to do.

b. UNICEF has had many successes, but it still has much work to do.

c. Despite having had many successes, UNICEF still has much work to do.

1. UNICEF spends most of its time on long-term projects. However, it still provides emergency help.

   a._____

   b._____

   c._____

2. UNICEF spends about half of its budget on care for young children. However, many children still die every year.

   a._____

   b._____

   c._____

j Writing

Think back to the chef in London who held an event called UNICHEF to raise money for UNICEF. Think of an event you could hold to raise money for UNICEF, using your special skills and talents. Write a description of the event, and then tell your classmates about it.

lesson
4

The Olympic Movement

© Eric Gaillard/Reuters/CORBIS

Before You Read

1. What is your opinion of the Olympic Games?

2. Who is responsible for organizing the Olympic Games?

3. What do you think the goal of the "Olympic Movement" is?

Context Clues

*The words in **bold** print below are from this lesson. Use context clues to guess what each word means.*

1. The Olympic Charter **guides** all decisions made about the Olympic Games.

2. The **judges** for Olympic events come from different countries. They often have very different opinions about the quality of an athlete's performance.

3. Members of a team usually have a sense of **solidarity** because they are working toward the same goal.

4. One goal of the Olympic Movement is to make people more **aware** of environmental problems.

5. You can **ponder** the problems for a while, but eventually you need to do something.

4 The Olympic Movement

The Olympic Movement **encompasses**
organizations, athletes, and other persons who agree to
be **guided** by the Olympic Charter.

includes

5 ## *Who Belongs to the Olympic Movement?*
The Olympic Movement groups together all those
who agree to be guided by the Olympic Charter and
who **recognize** the **authority** of the International
Olympic Committee (IOC)—namely, the International
10 Federations (IFs) of sports on the program of the
Olympic Games, the National Olympic Committees
(NOCs), the Organizing Committees of the Olympic
Games (OCOGs), athletes, **judges** and **referees**,
associations and clubs, as well as all the organizations
15 and institutions recognized by the IOC.

*experts who give
official opinions in
a competition*

Birth of the Olympic Movement
When he announced in Paris, on a winter's evening
in 1892, the **forthcoming** re-establishment of the Olympic
20 Games, Pierre de Coubertin was **applauded**, but nobody
at the time imagined the scale of the project **entailed** in
reviving the ancient Olympic Games, **appointing** a
committee in charge of organizing them, and creating an
international movement. The IOC was created on June
25 23, 1894; the first Olympic Games of the modern era
opened in Athens on April 6, 1896; and the Olympic
Movement has not stopped growing ever since.
Olympism is a **state of mind** based on equality of
sports which are international and **democratic**. It is a
30 **philosophy** of life, **exalting** and combining in a
balanced whole the qualities of body, will, and mind.

about to take place

*system of values by
which a person lives*

praising highly

Goals of the Olympic Movement
The goal of the Olympic Movement is to contribute
35 to building a peaceful and better world by educating
youth through sport practiced without discrimination of
any kind, in a spirit of friendship, **solidarity**, and fair

*feeling or state of
togetherness*

play. The Olympic Movement is defined also by the numerous activities in which it **engages**, such as

40 • Promoting sport and competitions through the **intermediary** of national and international sports institutions worldwide.

• <u>**Cooperation**</u> with public and private organizations to place sport at the service of mankind.

the act of working together

45 • Assistance to develop "Sport for All."

• Advancement of women in sport at all levels and in all structures, with a view to <u>**achieving**</u> equality between men and women.

reaching; arriving at

• Opposition to all forms of commercial **exploitation** of
50 sport and athletes.

unfair use

• The fight against doping.

• Promoting sports **ethics** and fair play.

• Raising **awareness** of environmental problems.

• Financial and educational support for developing
55 countries through the IOC institution Olympic Solidarity.

   "All sports for all people. This is surely a phrase that people will consider foolishly <u>**utopian**</u>. That prospect troubles me not at all. I have **pondered** and studied it at
60 length, and know that it is correct and possible," wrote Pierre de Coubertin in 1919. The future proved him right.

idealistic; wonderful but impossible

From http://www.olympic.org/uk/organisation/movement/index_uk.asp.
Reprinted with permission from the International Olympic Committee.

a   Vocabulary

encompasses	guide	authority	judge
referees	forthcoming	applauded	entail
state of mind	democratic	philosophy	exalted

1. What does becoming a doctor _____?
2. A delicious meal with friends always puts me in a good _____.
3. The UN peacekeeping forces do not have the _____ to enter into combat.
4. My history book _____ the 18th and 19th centuries only.
5. His _____ brings him peace of mind.
6. My cousin _____ high school basketball games.
7. In a _____ country, representatives are elected.
8. The school asked a professional musician to _____ the piano competition.
9. Dogs can be trained to _____ people who cannot see.
10. It was a great concert, and at the end people _____ for several minutes.
11. The coach _____ the winning runner, saying that she was the best athlete he had ever seen.
12. The author's last book was about cave painting, but his _____ book will be about ceramics.

b   Vocabulary

solidarity	engage	intermediary	cooperates
exploit	ethical	aware	utopian
pondered	achieve	appoints	recognize

1. Employers _____ their employees when they refuse to pay them what they deserve.
2. The president _____ his cabinet members. They are not elected.

89

3. The workers showed their _____ when they all refused to work for a day.

4. A world without wars and environmental problems is a _____ dream.

5. The UN sometimes acts as an _____ when two countries won't talk to each other.

6. I _____ the results of the study, but I couldn't explain them.

7. He didn't _____ me with my new haircut.

8. The committee members met for several hours, but they didn't _____ anything.

9. If everyone _____, we can get the job done quickly.

10. Some organizations _____ in only humanitarian activities.

11. Do you think it's _____ to take a sick day when you aren't sick?

12. Most people are _____ of the humanitarian crises in the world, but they don't want to think about them.

C Vocabulary Review: Odd One Out

Circle the word that doesn't fit in each group.

1. traumatize, identify, torture, abuse
2. award, eradicate, get rid of, eliminate
3. trial, judge, emergency, witness
4. donate, contribute, give, expand
5. global, forthcoming, international, worldwide
6. cooperation, malnutrition, contamination, discrimination
7. reliable, impartial, responsible, ignorant
8. incredible, arrogant, vast, extraordinary

d Comprehension Check: True/False/Not Enough Information

_____ 1. The IOC encompasses the International Federations and the National Olympic Committees.

_____ 2. Athletes are part of the Olympic Movement.

_____ 3. The ancient Olympic Games were revived in the 19th century.

_____ 4. The IOC was created to organize the modern Olympic Games.

_____ 5. The Olympic Movement's goal is to provide better sports programs for young people.

_____ 6. Both public and private organizations are involved in the Olympic Movement.

_____ 7. The Olympic Movement supports the commercial exploitation of athletes.

_____ 8. Pierre de Coubertin believed that the goals of the Olympic Movement were impossible to achieve.

e Comprehension Questions

1. Who belongs to the Olympic Movement?
2. What are the NOCs?
3. Who was Pierre de Coubertin?
4. When did the first modern Olympic Games take place?
5. What role did the IOC play in the first Olympic Games?
6. Do you agree that Olympism is a state of mind? Why or why not?
7. What is the main goal of the Olympic Movement and how does it plan to reach this goal?
8. What do you think "All sports for all people" means?
9. What is the Olympic Movement opposed to?

f　Reading Strategy: Inference

What can you infer from the sentences below? Check (✓) the possible inferences.

1. The Olympic Movement encompasses organizations, athletes, and other persons who agree to be guided by the Olympic Charter.

   ☐ The Olympic Movement is large.
   ☐ You don't have to be an athlete to be part of the Olympic Movement.
   ☐ The Olympic Movement is very old.
   ☐ It's expensive to be part of the Olympic Movement.

2. Olympism is a state of mind based on equality of sports which are international and democratic.

   ☐ Olympism is something new.
   ☐ Olympism is something you can do.
   ☐ Olympism does not approve of discrimination.
   ☐ Olympism is about the way you think.

3. When he announced in Paris, on a winter's evening in 1892, the forthcoming re-establishment of the Olympic Games, Pierre de Coubertin was applauded, but nobody at the time imagined the scale of the project entailed in reviving the ancient Olympic Games.

   ☐ People approved of Coubertin's idea of bringing back the Olympic Games.
   ☐ Coubertin established the first Olympic Games.
   ☐ Bringing back the Olympic Games was an enormous job.
   ☐ People knew how much work it would take to bring the Olympic Games back, but they wanted to do it anyway.

g Vocabulary Expansion: Word Forms

Choose the right word form for each sentence below.

	Verb	Noun	Adjective	Adverb
1.	guide	guide guidance		
2.	cooperate	cooperation	cooperative	cooperatively
3.	recognize	recognition	recognizable	
4.	exploit	exploitation	exploitable	
5.	applaud	applause		
6.	authorize	authority	authoritative	authoritatively
7.		ethics	ethical	ethically
8.	appoint	appointment		

1. If you need someone to _____ you around the city, you can pay for a tour _____.
2. The children wouldn't _____, so they weren't allowed to go outside.
3. With a wig on, she wasn't _____.
4. _____ of workers is unethical.
5. There was loud _____ at the end of the performance, and people continued to _____ for several minutes.
6. Who _____ closing down the road?
7. He had _____ reasons for quitting his job.
8. Her _____ as the new vice president will be forthcoming.

h Grammar Review: Verb Tenses

Complete the sentences with the correct form and tense of the verb in parentheses.

1. When Coubertin announced the re-establishment of the Olympic Games, people _____. (applaud)

2. The Olympic Movement _____ growing since 1896. (not stop)

3. Public and private organizations _____ to make the Olympic Games happen. (cooperate)

4. The Olympic Movement _____ all forms of commercial exploitation of sport. (oppose)

5. Pierre de Coubertin believed that it _____ possible for all sports to be for all people. (be)

6. In the 1890s, no one _____ how much work would be involved in re-establishing the Olympic Games. (recognize)

7. In June 1894, the IOC _____. (create)

8. The Olympic Charter _____ everyone involved in the Olympic Movement. (encompass)

i Sentence Combining

Read the example and the model combinations below. Then rewrite sentences 1 and 2 following the models.

Example: Olympism is a philosophy of life. It exalts and combines the qualities of body, will, and mind.

Models: a. Olympism is a philosophy of life, exalting and combining the qualities of body, will, and mind.
　　　　 b. Olympism, which is a philosophy of life, exalts and combines the qualities of body, will, and mind.
　　　　 c. Olympism is a philosophy of life that exalts and combines the qualities of body, will, and mind.

1. The IOC is an important part of the Olympic Movement. It chooses the site of the Olympic Games.

   a. _____

   b. _____

   c. _____

2. The Olympic Movement is involved in many activities. It promotes sports and raises awareness of environmental problems.

   a. _____

   b. _____

   c. _____

j Writing

Write a description of your favorite Olympic event, but do not write the name of the event. Then ask another student to read your description and guess the event.

95

Video Highlights

a Before You Watch

1. Think back to the lessons on the United Nations and UNICEF, and answer the questions.
   a. Why was the UN formed?
   b. Why was UNICEF formed?
   c. How do you think the UN Children's Forum might be related to these two organizations?
2. The words below are from this unit. Can you remember what they mean?

issues	accurate	representatives	responsibility
global	focus	specific	vital
awareness	delegates	recognize	population

b As You Watch

1. Five of the words above are used in the video. Circle the words that you think will be used. Then watch the video to see how these words are used. What is the context?
2. Watch the video again. Take notes, and answer the questions below.

   a. Why did the UN decide to hold a children's forum?

   _____

   _____

   b. Who can participate? How?

   _____

   _____

   c. Where can you go to find more information?

   _____

   _____

C   After You Watch

1. Imagine you are 17 years old and have been invited to be a delegate to the UN Children's Forum. What issues would you focus on? List your top three issues.

   _____

   _____

   _____

2. In groups, discuss your individual issues. As a group, decide which three issues are the most important and why they should be top priorities.

Issue	Reasons why it's important

3. Present your group's issues to the class, using the vocabulary in the list. Take a vote of the class to determine what the top issues are.

Activity Page

Crossword Puzzle

[Crossword grid with numbered squares 1–18]

Across

2. You look so different with contact lenses that I almost didn't _____ you.
7. Tsunamis, earthquakes, floods, and tornadoes are natural _____.
8. job or position
10. We should allow some extra money for transportation in this month's _____.
11. chosen by the people
14. The _____ FBI stands for Federal Bureau of Investigation.
15. Murder can carry a _____ of life in prison.
16. correct
17. detailed, explicit
18. the opposite of knowledge

Down

1. One of the major goals of Amnesty International is to ensure that prisoners receive a _____ trial.
3. The acronym UNICEF stands for United Nations International Children's _____ Fund.
4. beliefs about right and wrong
5. worth a lot
6. The UN has organized committees to address a variety of global _____.
9. working together
12. having to do with money
13. to think long and hard about something very serious

98

Understanding Acronyms

An acronym is an expression formed from the first letters of other words.

1. Use your dictionary to find the full name for each of the acronyms in the chart and what the organization does.

Acronym	Full name	What it does
FBI	*Federal Bureau of Investigation*	*investigates national crimes*
CIA		
NAACP		
NASA		
IRS		
NOW		
UN		
EU		
NASDAQ		
YMCA		
NATO		

2. Complete the chart with acronyms from above.

Government organizations	Nongovernment organizations
FBI	

Places

*The place honors not the man; it is the man
who honors the place.*
—**Hebrew proverb**

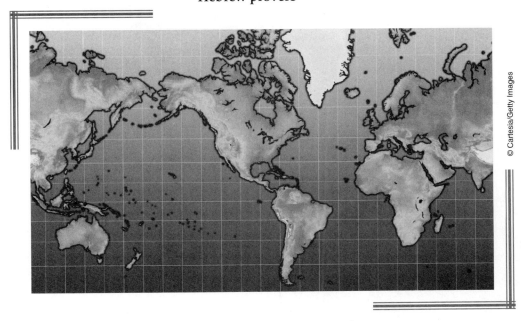

© Cartesia/Getty Images

Hawaii

© tomas del amo/Alamy

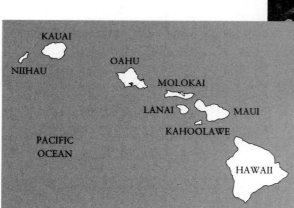

Before You Read

1. Have you ever been to Hawaii?

2. What are three facts you know about Hawaii?

3. What would you expect to find on these islands?

Context Clues

*The words in **bold** print below are from this lesson. Use context clues to guess what each word means.*

1. Many years ago, the island of Kahoolawe was covered with **vegetation**; today there is nothing growing on it.

2. European settlers brought **grazing** animals to the island. When the animals finished eating all of the vegetation, nothing remained to protect the soil from the wind.

3. Many of the people on the island suffered from Hansen's disease, **formerly** known as leprosy.

4. In the 1820s, **missionaries** from the United States arrived to teach the Hawaiian people about Christianity.

1   Hawaii

   If you travel 3,700 kilometers southwest from Los Angeles across the Pacific Ocean, you will reach the islands of Hawaii, the 50th state of the United States. This group of islands has a land area of only 16,700
5 square kilometers, stretched over 2,500 kilometers of ocean. The eight main Hawaiian Islands are Niihau, Lanai, Kauai, Maui, Oahu, Molokai, Kahoolawe, and the Big Island of Hawaii.
   Not all of the Hawaiian Islands are popular **tourist**
10 spots. In fact, one of them is **uninhabitable** and **off-limits** to tourists. That's the island of Kahoolawe, the smallest of the Hawaiian Islands. Many years ago, this island was covered with **vegetation**; today it is <u>barren</u>   without life
   and **inhospitable**. The <u>blame</u> for this goes first to   responsibility for
15 European settlers who brought **grazing** animals to the   something bad
   island. When the animals finished eating all of the vegetation, nothing remained to protect the soil from

the Pacific winds. It's possible that as much as 2 million metric tons of soil gets blown off the island each year.

20 Kahoolawe was also used as a **target** by the U.S. Navy, and today there are still enough unexploded shells on the ground to **discourage** even the most **foolhardy** tourist. At present, the island is being restored, and scientists hope that someday Kahoolawe will be the

25 beautiful place it once was.

A second rarely visited part of Hawaii is the island of Niihau, which is known as "The Forbidden Island." This privately owned island has fewer than 250 inhabitants, and you need an invitation from one of

30 them to be allowed onto the island. The owner of Niihau raises cattle on his <u>secluded</u> ranch, and many of   **hidden** the people on the island work for him. People say that there is no electricity on the island and that the inhabitants have chosen to live in the traditional way in

35 order to preserve traditional Hawaiian culture.

The remaining six Hawaiian Islands are open to tourists, though three of them attract far fewer tourists than the others. Molokai is home to more **native** Hawaiians than any other island. This island **boasts** the

40 highest sea cliffs in the world and a wildlife park with rare animals from Africa and India. For many years, Molokai was one of the most beautiful "prisons" in the world. From 1865 to 1969, more than 8,000 people were sent to this island. But the only <u>crime</u> these people had   **a bad thing;**

45 **committed** was to suffer from Hansen's disease   **illegal act** (**formerly** known as leprosy). Until a treatment for the disease was discovered in the late 1940s, anyone **suspected** of carrying the disease was sent to live in isolation on Molokai. Molokai is also home to the

50 Kalokeoli Fishpond, which is an example of the sophisticated aquaculture used on the island at least 700 years ago.

South of Molokai lies the island of Lanai. Lanai is a relatively dry island because the mountains on Molokai

55 block the rain clouds from reaching the island. That doesn't mean Lanai is barren and **infertile**. Today, one-fifth of all Hawaiian pineapples come from this

104

island. The island of Kauai has the honor of being one of the wettest places on Earth, with an average of 1,240 centimeters of rain per year.

The remaining three islands, Oahu, Maui, and Hawaii, are all popular destinations for tourists. With its wonderful surfing, beaches, and golf courses, Oahu **draws** the most tourists of all. Oahu also has the only royal palace in the United States and the largest wind generator in the world. The island of Maui draws visitors who want to see the world's largest inactive volcano, while the most daring tourists travel to the island of Hawaii, which has the world's most active volcano. Hawaii is also the largest island in the group. In fact, Hawaii is twice the size of the other seven islands combined. Hawaii also produces some of the world's best coffee and macadamia nuts and one-third of the world's supply of pineapples.

Of all the states in the United States, Hawaii has perhaps the most **ethnically diverse** population, and that may be a result of the way in which the islands were settled. The first people to make their home on the Hawaiian Islands sailed there from other Pacific islands between the years 300 and 600. Much later, the English explorer and mapmaker Captain James Cook sailed to the Hawaiian Islands. In 1778, Cook put the islands on his maps, and before long whaling ships were stopping there for supplies. In the 1820s, **missionaries** from the United States arrived to teach the Hawaiian people about Christianity. Some of the missionaries settled there permanently and started farms to grow sugar and, later, pineapples. As the farms grew and more farm workers were needed, the farm owners brought in workers from other countries. In 1852, workers arrived from China, followed by an **influx** of Japanese workers in 1868 and workers from the Philippines in 1906. Later, people from Korea, Portugal, and Puerto Rico came to work on the farms. Over time, people from the different ethnic groups intermarried, handing down a rich mix of cultures to their children and grandchildren. For example, a Hawaiian child might have a Chinese-

attracts

varied

arrival of a large number of people

Lesson 1: Hawaii

Hawaiian mother and a Portuguese-Filipino father. Today, about 1.2 million people live in Hawaii, but
100 only 10,000 are native Hawaiians.

Hawaii is known as the Aloha State. *Aloha* means "hello," "good-bye," and "I love you" in Hawaiian. It's a word the average tourist is likely to say many times while visiting the Hawaiian Islands.

a Vocabulary

tourists	missionaries	uninhabitable	influx
vegetation	barren	formerly	blamed
graze	discouraging	foolhardy	target

1. When gold was first discovered in California, there was an _____ of people who hoped to find some gold for themselves.

2. Every city has attractions for _____ that the local people rarely visit.

3. Nothing can grow on that _____ land.

4. The moon is _____ because it doesn't have oxygen.

5. They got _____ for committing the crime even though they didn't do it.

6. Only a _____ person would do something so dangerous.

7. Many religions send out _____ to teach other people their beliefs.

8. We hope to finish our work by the 15th of the month. That's our _____ date.

9. It's _____ to never succeed at anything.

10. The Hawaiian Islands were _____ called the Sandwich Islands.

11. You need a lot of land if you are going to let your horses _____ outdoors.

12. During the winter the land is bare, but in the summer thick _____ covers the ground.

b Vocabulary

secluded	native	boast	off-limits
crime	commit	inhospitable	suspect
infertile	draws	ethnic	diverse

1. Vandalism is a _____ in most places.
2. What is the worst crime a person can _____?
3. The president's office is _____ to most people.
4. You cannot grow anything from _____ seeds.
5. What plants are _____ to your area?
6. Young children like to _____ that they are very strong or very smart.
7. For some people, the excessive rain in Kauai makes it an _____ place to live.
8. You won't get a lot of visitors if you live in a very _____ area.
9. There are a lot of _____ restaurants on Oahu, so you can try foods from many different cultures.
10. I _____ that these pineapples are from Hawaii, but I'm not certain.
11. The people in my class were from _____ backgrounds.
12. The great weather _____ a lot of tourists to Hawaii.

c Vocabulary Review: Definitions

Match the words with their definitions.

_____ 1. ponder   a. say
_____ 2. forthcoming   b. do something unfair
_____ 3. remark   c. get rid of
_____ 4. eradicate   d. direct someone or something
_____ 5. cheat   e. take advantage of
_____ 6. malnutrition   f. donate something
_____ 7. guide   g. think about
_____ 8. exploit   h. give money to
                           i. a condition resulting from a lack of good food
                           j. soon to arrive

d | Comprehension Check: True/False/Not Enough Information

_____ 1. Hawaii became the 50th state in the United States in 1959.

_____ 2. All of the main Hawaiian Islands are off-limits to tourists.

_____ 3. The island of Niihau was used for target practice by the U.S. Navy.

_____ 4. It's dangerous to walk on the island of Kahoolawe.

_____ 5. You need special permission to visit the island of Oahu.

_____ 6. The island of Molokai is now a settlement for people with Hansen's disease.

_____ 7. Kauai gets more rain than most places on Earth.

_____ 8. The island that attracts the most tourists is Oahu.

_____ 9. Early inhabitants of Molokai were very inventive.

_____ 10. Missionaries came to the Hawaiian Islands from all parts of the world.

e | Comprehension Questions

1. Where are the Hawaiian Islands?
2. Why is the island of Kahoolawe barren and inhospitable?
3. How is Niihau different from the other main islands?
4. If you wanted to see an active volcano, which island would you visit?
5. Why does Lanai get so little rain?
6. What role did Captain Cook play in the history of Hawaii?
7. Why is the population of Hawaii so ethnically diverse?
8. Which island is the most interesting to you and why?

f Reading Strategy: Making a Timeline

Timelines are charts showing when important events or activities took place.

This timeline shows the years of several important events in the history of Hawaii. Look at the reading again to find the event that happened each year. Then write the event next to the year.

First
settlers
arrived

300	1300	1778	1820	1852	1865	1868	1906

g Vocabulary Expansion: Suffixes

You can add a suffix to some verbs to make a noun.

Look at the chart below and circle the suffix that was added to make each noun. Choose the correct form of the word to complete each question, and then answer the questions.

	Verb	Noun
1.	attract	attraction
2.	commit	commitment
3.	discourage	discouragement
4.	inhabit	inhabitant
5.	vegetate	vegetation
6.	combine	combination
7.	preserve	preservation

1. What would _____ you to Hawaii?
2. What types of _____ do people make during their life?
3. How could you _____ a young person from vandalizing something?
4. How many _____ does your city have?
5. Why do some people like to _____ all day?

109

6. What foods do you think are a good _____?
7. Would you be willing to donate money for the _____ of natural landscapes?

h Grammar Review: Noun Substitutes

*Read these groups of sentences and study the pronouns in **bold** print. Circle the noun or noun phrase that each pronoun replaces.*

1. Not all of the Hawaiian Islands are popular tourists spots. In fact, one of **them** is uninhabitable.
2. Many years ago, this island was covered with vegetation; today, **it** is barren and inhospitable.
3. This privately owned island has fewer than 250 inhabitants, and you need an invitation from one of **them** to be allowed onto the island.
4. The owner of Niihau raises cattle on his secluded ranch, and many of the people on the island work for **him**.
5. With **its** wonderful surfing, beaches, and golf courses, Oahu draws the most tourists of all.

i Sentence Combining

Read the example and the model combinations below. Then rewrite sentences 1 and 2 following the models.

Example: Molokai is home to the Kalokeoli Fishpond. It's an example of the sophisticated aquaculture used a long time ago.

Models: a. Molokai is home to the Kalokeoli Fishpond, which is an example of the sophisticated aquaculture used a long time ago.
b. Molokai is home to the Kalokeoli Fishpond, an example of the sophisticated aquaculture used a long time ago.
c. Kalokeoli Fishpond, which is on the island of Molokai, is an example of the sophisticated aquaculture used a long time ago.

1. Hawaii is home to Mt. Kilauea. It's the most active volcano in the world.

   a. _____

   b. _____

   c. _____

2. Oahu is home to the Iolani Palace. It's the only royal palace in the United States.

a. _____

b. _____

c. _____

 Writing

Choose a place you know well. In the chart below, list several facts and opinions about the place. Then use the information in your chart to write a short description of the place for your classmates to read.

Name of Place: _____

Facts	Opinions

lesson

2

Deserts

© Robert Francis/Getty Images

Before You Read

1. How would you describe a desert?

2. What kinds of plants and animals live in deserts?

3. Can you think of some countries that have deserts?

Context Clues

*The words in **bold** print below are from this lesson. Use context clues to guess what each word means.*

1. There is nothing **static** about deserts. The sizes and locations of the world's deserts are always changing.

2. One area's **gain** is another area's loss.

3. Trees and other vegetation acted as a **barrier** between the Taklimakan and Kumtag deserts.

4. Today, roughly 135 million people are at risk of losing their land to desertification and becoming **refugees**.

2   Deserts

They are some of the coldest places on Earth and some of the hottest. They exist on every continent except Europe, and together they cover roughly one-third of the land on Earth. We call them deserts, and
5   they all have one thing in common—they get less than 250 millimeters of rain a year.

The world's largest and hottest desert spreads across North Africa from the Red Sea to the Atlantic Ocean, covering more than 9 million square kilometers. It's
10 called the Sahara, which means "**wilderness**" in Arabic.   **land unspoiled by humans**
But the Sahara was not always a barren wilderness. At one time, it was an area of **lush** vegetation with huge river systems; cave paintings found in the area reveal that elephants, giraffes, and other animals once
15 lived there.

There is nothing **static** about deserts. The sizes and locations of the world's deserts are always changing. Over millions of years, as the climate changed and mountains rose, new dry areas developed. But within
20 the last 100 years, deserts have been growing at a

  113

frightening speed. This is **due**, in part, **to** climate change, but the greatest desert makers of all are humans.

because of; a result of

25 The process of turning productive land into desert-like land is called desertification. Desertification **takes place** slowly as small pieces of **degraded** land spread and **merge** together. Desertification can take place naturally on the edges of existing deserts, or it can start in small patches hundreds of miles away from the
30 nearest desert. When there is a **drought**, for example, the winds and high temperatures dry the soil out. Eventually, the topsoil is blown or washed away, and nothing can grow in the area. Unfortunately, these natural processes are greatly **accelerated** by the
35 activities of human beings.

happens

speeded up

The human activity most destructive to the soil is overgrazing. When there are too many animals eating the vegetation in an area, the root systems of the plants are destroyed and the soil is left without a protective
40 cover. The unprotected soil can then be easily **eroded**. Any land that is cleared of vegetation becomes **vulnerable** to desertification.

A second cause of desertification is improper irrigation. Farmers in many parts of the world **divert**
45 water supplies for their crops. However, one area's **gain** is another area's loss. In China's Xinjiang Autonomous Region, for example, the building of dams and the withdrawal of water for irrigation have dried up the Tarim River. This has caused the trees and other
50 vegetation that acted as a **barrier** between the Taklimakan and Kumtag deserts to die off. Now the two deserts are spreading toward each other, and they may eventually merge.

Deforestation also contributes **significantly** to
55 desertification. In developing countries, 90 percent of the people use wood for cooking and heating. However, cutting down trees for firewood leaves the land exposed to the sun. The smaller plants that grow under the trees cannot survive without the shade of
60 the trees. And without leaves from the trees to enrich

a lot; noticeably

114

it, the soil becomes poor and deprived of nutrients.
Eventually, the smaller plants die, and nothing
remains but barren land. Oftentimes, the soil is so
degraded that it becomes as hard as concrete. Large
65 pieces of land cleared to grow crops can become
useless in just a few seasons.

While humans have shown themselves to be **adept**   good
at making deserts, they can also stop their spread and
even **reclaim** the land. In 1977, the United Nations
70 invited representatives from around the world to a
conference on desertification. The members of the
conference came up with a plan to stop or reduce
desertification and to reclaim the degraded land. They
also designated June 17 as World Day to Combat
75 Desertification and Drought. It is part of a United
Nations campaign to make people more aware of
land degradation.

Some of the methods for stopping the advance of
deserts are quite simple. Algeria, for example, has
80 planted a green wall of trees across the edge of the
Sahara to prevent more land from turning into desert.
Mauritania planted a similar wall around Nouakchott,
its capital. In Kenya, farmers have planted more than 7
million trees around croplands to reduce wind erosion.
85 And now the Chinese government has started the
world's largest tree planting project—a green wall
that will stretch for more than 5,700 kilometers.
In Iran, people put a thin layer of petroleum on the
dry land to help the land hold water and newly
90 planted vegetation.

To stop the overgrazing of land, some areas are
requiring the careful **management** of **livestock**, while   farm animals such
other areas have gone so far as to **ban** the grazing of   as cattle, pigs, and
certain kinds of animals on open land. To combat   chickens
95 deforestation, people are being encouraged to use   prohibit; refuse to
alternative methods of heating and cooking. Simple   allow
devices such as solar cookers and wind turbines can
help to reduce people's dependence on wood.

Despite these efforts, the rate of desertification has
100 doubled since the 1970s. Just since 1990, it is estimated

115

that roughly 6 million hectares of productive land has
been degraded each year. Today, roughly 135 million
people are at risk of losing their land to desertification
and becoming **refugees**. Perhaps UN spokesman
105 Michel Smitall described the situation best when he
said, "It's a creeping **catastrophe**. Entire parts of the
world might become uninhabitable."

a Vocabulary

wilderness	lush	static	due to
take place	degraded	merge	drought
accelerate	vulnerable	diverted	gain

1. Several bad accidents that happened last week were _____
   to the icy roads.
2. In rainy climates, there is _____ vegetation.
3. As people get older and become less active, they often
   _____ weight.
4. There are no roads through a _____ area.
5. Cars _____ when drivers push on the gas pedal.
6. While the road was being fixed, the police _____ all traffic
   onto a parallel street.
7. During times of _____, people have to travel in search of
   water.
8. _____ land cannot be used for agriculture.
9. The traffic is always bad where the two highways _____
   just outside the city.
10. The food supply was _____ for several years, but then it
    dropped suddenly.
11. Erosion starts to _____ as soon as land loses its vegetation.
12. Without immunization, children are _____ to a number of
    diseases.

b Vocabulary

barrier	significant	adept	reclaim
erosion	management	livestock	banned
despite	gain	refugees	catastrophe

1. Thousands of people help with the _____ of the United Nations.
2. It was a pretty quiet trip; nothing _____ happened.
3. Cattle, pigs, and goats are examples of _____.
4. The police put a _____ across the road to stop the traffic.
5. The land around the house is in such terrible condition that it will take years to _____ it.
6. You can stop _____ by planting trees.
7. Tourists are _____ from visiting the island of Kahoolawe because there are still unexploded shells on the ground.
8. The war was a _____ for everyone involved.
9. He wore a coat _____ the hot weather.
10. Doctors need to be _____ at giving shots.
11. The United Nations tries to provide temporary facilities for _____ of war.

c Vocabulary Review: Antonyms

Match the antonyms.

_____ 1. off-limits	a. similar
_____ 2. barren	b. decrease
_____ 3. diverse	c. fail
_____ 4. impartial	d. eradicate
_____ 5. expand	e. accessible
_____ 6. achieve	f. imprison
_____ 7. focus on	g. loss
_____ 8. accurate	h. unfair
_____ 9. gain	i. ignore
_____ 10. release	j. wrong
	k. lush

d Comprehension Check: Multiple Choice

Circle the letter of the best answer.

1. All deserts get less than _____ millimeters of rain a year.
   a. 25
   b. 250
   c. 2,500

2. Today, the amount of desert on Earth is _____.
   a. decreasing
   b. increasing slowly
   c. increasing rapidly

3. Natural processes and _____ cause desertification.
   a. human activities
   b. droughts
   c. winds

4. The Tarim River in China dried up because _____.
   a. there was a drought
   b. a barrier was built between the two deserts
   c. water was diverted for irrigation

5. The first UN conference on desertification took place in _____.
   a. 1977
   b. 1985
   c. 1990

6. In _____, a wall of trees has been planted around the capital of the country.
   a. Algeria
   b. Mauritania
   c. Kenya

7. To stop _____, some countries are encouraging people to use solar power.
   a. overgrazing
   b. deforestation
   c. the diversion of water

8. You could say that desertification is a _____ problem today than it was 30 years ago.
   a. more serious
   b. less serious
   c. less understood

e Comprehension Questions

1. How would you define a desert?
2. What is unique about the Sahara Desert?
3. What is desertification?
4. What are some natural causes of desertification?
5. How does overgrazing affect the land?
6. Why is cleared land vulnerable to desertification?
7. What negative effects did the diversion of water from the Tarim River in China have?
8. Why is deforestation happening so quickly?
9. What can people use for heating and cooking instead of wood?
10. What are some ways to stop the process of desertification?
11. Do you agree with Michel Smitall's opinion of desertification? Why or why not?

f Reading Strategy: Identifying Cause and Effect

When you read a text that gives the causes and effects of something, you can improve your understanding by making a cause and effect chain with information from the text.

In the two chains below, add the missing information.

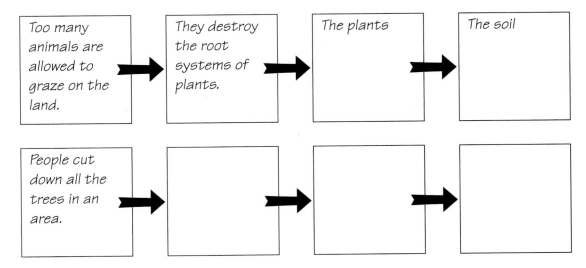

g Vocabulary Expansion: Collocations

Look back over the reading on pages 113–116 to find another word to add to each list below.

1. Things you can **clear**: the table, the room, _____
2. Things you can **grow**: food, flowers, _____
3. Things you can **reduce**: the spread of a disease, _____
4. Things that can **merge**: two roads, two rivers, two _____
5. Things that you can **plant**: flowers, _____

h Grammar Review: Prepositions

Write the missing prepositions on the lines.

To stop the overgrazing (1) _____ land, some areas are requiring the careful management (2) _____ livestock, while other areas have gone so far as to ban the grazing (3) _____ certain kinds of animals (4) _____ open land. To combat deforestation, people are being encouraged to use alternative methods (5) _____ heating and cooking. Simple devices such as solar cookers and wind turbines can help to reduce people's dependence (6) _____ wood.

Sentence Combining

Read the example and the model combinations below. Then rewrite sentences 1 and 2 following the models.

Example: Large pieces of land are cleared to grow crops. In just a few seasons, the land becomes useless.

Models: a. Large pieces of land are cleared to grow crops, but in just a few seasons the land becomes useless.
   b. Large pieces of land cleared to grow crops become useless in just a few seasons.
   c. When large pieces of land are cleared to grow crops, the land becomes useless in just a few seasons.

1. Rivers are diverted to irrigate crops. Before long, the rivers dry up.

   a. _____
   b. _____
   c. _____

2. Animals are allowed to graze on the land. They destroy the root systems of plants.

   a. _____
   b. _____
   c. _____

 Writing

Choose one of the activities below or think of one of your own:
   driving cars   exploring space   learning foreign languages
   watching TV   killing insects   hosting the Olympic Games

Make a cause and effect chain identifying the effects of this activity. Then summarize your ideas in a paragraph for your classmates to read.

lesson 3

Antarctica

© Kim Westerskov/Getty Images

Before You Read

1. What is the climate like in Antarctica?

2. What kinds of animals live there?

3. What kinds of research do you think scientists are doing there?

Context Clues

*The words in **bold** print below are from this lesson. Use context clues to guess what each word means.*

1. Walking 2,700 kilometers across Antarctica is no easy **feat**.

2. While the surface of Antarctica is inhospitable to most living things, the water surrounding the continent is **teeming** with living creatures.

3. In 1959, the Antarctic **Treaty** established Antarctica as a special area to be governed internationally and used for scientific research.

4. The few scientists who remain in Antarctica for the winter have only radios, phones, and the Internet to **link** them to the rest of the world. After six or seven months, a plane returns with supplies and releases the scientists from their **solitude**.

3   Antarctica

    In 2001, Ann Bancroft and Liv Arnesen traveled 2,700 kilometers on foot across Antarctica, each pulling a sled carrying 100 kilograms of food and equipment. Crossing this land of **extremes** was no easy **feat**. The
5 temperature in Antarctica is often an **unimaginable** −40°C—the temperature at which skin and <u>flesh</u> freeze! Antarctica holds the record for the coldest temperature ever measured on Earth, which is −89.2°C.

    Antarctica contains **approximately** 70 percent of the
10 world's fresh water supply, and yet it is considered to be one of the world's largest deserts. That's because Antarctica's **enormous** supply of fresh water is locked up in ice that averages over two kilometers in thickness. If the ice sheets melted, the seas would rise as much as
15 60 meters. However, like all other deserts on Earth,

the soft substance beneath the skin

Antarctica receives less than 250 millimeters of rain a year. It's hard to believe that, 500 million years ago, Antarctica had a warm climate and a cover of lush vegetation.

20   Despite the enormous size of the continent, only a few **invertebrates** can survive on the Antarctic **peninsula**, and even they are rare. The largest of this group is a type of midge, which grows to the **colossal** size of 12 millimeters. The only plant life that can
25   survive in this harsh climate consists mainly of algae, moss, and lichen.

animals without backbones

a long strip of land surrounded by water and connected to the mainland

huge (used sarcastically here to mean very small)

While the surface of Antarctica is inhospitable to most living things, the water surrounding the continent is **teeming** with living creatures. At the bottom of the
30   **food chain** in Antarctic waters is a **hardy** type of algae. During the winter, the algae live between the layers of snow on the sea ice, but when the ice breaks open in the spring, the algae pour into the ocean. Huge numbers of krill, tiny sea animals that are less than eight
35   centimeters long, feed on the algae. The krill, **in turn**, are a vital source of food for seabirds, fish, seals, whales, and penguins.

succession of organisms, each of which uses the next lower member of the sequence as a food source

in sequence

Animals are not the only creatures drawn to the land of extremes. In 1959, the Antarctic **Treaty** established
40   Antarctica as a special area to be governed internationally and used for scientific research. The treaty declared, "It is in the interest of all mankind that Antarctica shall continue to be used **forever** for peaceful purposes and shall not become the **scene** or object of
45   international **discord**."

disagreement; conflict

Today, Antarctica has more than 30 research stations, including those of Argentina, Australia, Chile, Germany, Great Britain, Italy, Japan, New Zealand, Russia, and the United States. Most scientists live and work there from
50   October to March, when the sun shines 24 hours a day. The second half of the year brings darkness and isolation. The few scientists who remain are trapped for months with only radios, phones, and the Internet to **link** them to the rest of the world. After six or seven

55 months, a plane returns with supplies and releases the
scientists from their **solitude**.

Scientists know that this huge, icy area holds
important information about the planet. Their research
has already shown that Antarctica plays a crucial role in
60 the production of the cold deep water responsible for
the **circulation** of water in the oceans. They also know
that Antarctica holds the largest supply of fresh water
on Earth. Much of their research focuses on ozone, a
form of oxygen. The ozone layer protects living things
65 from the dangerous rays of the Sun. In the mid-1980s,
scientists discovered that the ozone layer above
Antarctica was very thin.

Scientists have also discovered that the temperature
of the air and the water in Antarctica has been slowly
70 rising since 1970. Warmer temperatures result in less sea
ice during the winter months, and this may be having an
effect on the Antarctic food chain. Scientists know that
the number of krill in ocean waters near the Antarctic
peninsula has **declined** about 80 percent since the 1970s.
75 The most likely explanation is the decline in the amount
of winter sea ice and the algae that live on it.

Humans are also affecting the food chain in
Antarctica as they start **harvesting** krill in greater and
greater numbers. It turns out that krill is a useful
80 ingredient in a number of products. For example,
it's used to make **cosmetics**, contact lenses, **artificial**
skin, and specialized cleaning supplies. Other
natural resources in Antarctica are being similarly
exploited **commercially**.
85 Scientists will continue to study penguin and krill
populations and carefully watch the ozone layer above
Antarctica and the ice in the seas. If we are smart, we
will protect the Antarctic environment that is so vital to
our own well-being.

movement (of something) in a circular path

beauty preparations used often on the face

a Vocabulary

extremely	feat	flesh	unimaginable
enormous	peninsula	artificial	approximately
teeming	food chain	hardy	invertebrate

1. People eat the _____ of animals, not the bones.
2. Asia is an _____ continent, while Australia is quite small.
3. A _____ plant can grow just about anywhere.
4. With temperatures of −40°C, Antarctica is an _____ cold place.
5. If you live on a _____, you have water on three sides.
6. During the summer, the air is _____ with insects.
7. Making his or her nation's Olympic team is an amazing _____ for any athlete.
8. The way we live today would have been _____ 200 years ago.
9. Krill are an important part of the Antarctic _____. Without krill to eat, many larger animals would starve to death.
10. An _____ tree doesn't require any water.
11. An insect is an example of an _____, but a mouse is not.
12. I don't know exactly what the temperature is, but I think it's _____ 10°C.

b Vocabulary

colossal	in turn	treaty	forever
scene	discord	link	solitude
circulate	decline	harvest	cosmetics

1. If you need a lot of _____, you should probably move into the countryside.
2. The police immediately went to the _____ of the crime to look for clues.
3. The _____ industry makes a lot of money on face creams and lipstick.

126

4. Allowing animals to graze on the land was a _____ mistake because it killed the vegetation.
5. It's important to _____ crops before wild animal eat them.
6. Romeo asked a question, and Juliet _____ answered it.
7. Doctors know that there is a _____ between smoking and cancer.
8. Nothing remains the same _____.
9. Unfortunately, _____ between two countries can lead to war.
10. It sometimes takes years of negotiation to get countries to sign a

    _____.
11. A _____ in the value of money can make it difficult for people to buy things.
12. They used a fan to _____ the heat around the house.

c Vocabulary Review: Synonyms

Match the synonyms.

_____ 1. static   a. bold
_____ 2. adept   b. gain
_____ 3. daring   c. send
_____ 4. ban   d. forbid
_____ 5. achieve   e. happen
_____ 6. transmit   f. merge
_____ 7. due to   g. unchanging
_____ 8. take place   h. crime
                           i. because of
                           j. good at

d Comprehension Check: True/False/Not Enough Information

_____ 1. It's colder in the Arctic than in Antarctica.
_____ 2. Flesh freezes at −89.2°C.
_____ 3. Even though there is a lot of water in Antarctica, it is a very dry place.

_____ 4. Many different kinds of invertebrates live in Antarctica.

_____ 5. A midge is a kind of invertebrate.

_____ 6. Algae feed on krill.

_____ 7. Penguins feed on krill.

_____ 8. No one stays in Antarctica year-round.

_____ 9. The air temperature in Antarctica is going up.

_____10. There are more krill in the water surrounding Antarctica than there used to be.

e   Comprehension Questions

1. What are three things that make Antarctica unique?
2. What kinds of living things survive in and around Antarctica?
3. What is the food chain in the water surrounding Antarctica?
4. What is the purpose of the Antarctic Treaty?
5. How would you describe a scientist's life in Antarctica in the winter?
6. What effect does the cold deep water around Antarctica have on other oceans?
7. What effects are the rising air and water temperatures having on the food chain in Antarctica?
8. What can krill be used for?

f   Reading Strategy: Using Context Clues

Many words in English have more than one meaning. As you read, it's important to use context clues (the surrounding words and ideas) to guess the correct meaning of words.

Read the definitions of each word below. Then use context clues to guess the meaning of the word in each context. Write the letter of the definition.

bold
a daring; courageous
b impolite; too direct
c distinct; clear

_____ 1. They chose a **bold** design for the building because they wanted it to stand out.

_____ 2. It takes a **bold** person to sail alone around the world.

_____ 3. Entering without knocking was a **bold** thing for him to do.

128

moved
a changed the position of
b sold
c affected emotionally

_____ 4. The story she told **moved** everyone in the room.

_____ 5. When the store reduced its prices, everything **moved** quickly.

_____ 6. They **moved** all the furniture out of the room before painting it.

static
a _adjective_ not moving; not changing
b _noun_ crackling noise on the radio or TV caused by electrical problems or interference

_____ 7. We couldn't hear his voice above the **static**.

_____ 8. The number of animals in the area has remained **static**.

extreme
a farthest away
b radical; very different from what most people think
c very great

_____ 9. They live at the **extreme** end of the road.

_____ 10. Choosing to live in a cave is a pretty **extreme** idea.

_____ 11. The publisher put **extreme** pressure on the writer to finish the book quickly.

 g Vocabulary Expansion: Word Forms

Choose the right word form for each sentence below.

	Verb	Noun	Adjective	Adverb
1.	imagine	imagination	(un)imaginable	(un)imaginably
2.	circulate	circulation	circulatory	circularly
3.		extreme	extreme	extremely
4.	link	link, linkage		
5.		artifice	artificial	artificially
6.	erode	erosion		

1. If you can _____ yourself living thousands of years ago, then you must have a good _____.

2. Your blood _____ inside your body. If you have cold feet and hands, you might have bad _____.

3. Antarctica is at one _____ of planet Earth, while the Arctic is at the other.

4. Is there any _____ between the decreasing amount of sea ice and the decreasing number of krill?

5. Today, you can participate in sports even if you have an _____ knee or hip.

6. Too much rain can cause serious problems with _____.

h Grammar Review: Articles

Put an article in each blank if one is necessary.

Despite (1) _____ enormous size of (2) _____ continent, only a few invertebrates can survive on (3) _____ Antarctic peninsula, and even they are (4) _____ rare. The largest of this group is (5) _____ type of midge, which grows to the colossal size of 12 millimeters. (6) _____ only plant life that can survive in this harsh climate consists mainly of (7) _____ algae, moss, and lichen.

While (8) _____ surface of Antarctica is inhospitable to most living things, the water surrounding (9) _____ continent is teeming with (10) _____ living creatures. At the bottom of the food chain in Antarctic waters is (11) _____ hardy type of algae. During the winter, (12) _____ algae live between the layers of snow on the sea ice, but when (13) _____ ice breaks open in the spring, the algae pour into the ocean. Huge numbers of krill, tiny sea animals that are less than eight centimeters long, feed on (14) _____ algae. The krill, in turn, are (15) _____ vital source of food for seabirds, fish, seals, whales, and penguins.

i Sentence Combining

Read the examples and the model combinations below. Then rewrite sentences 1 to 4 following the models.

Example: Antarctica is a desert. Deserts receive less than 250 millimeters of rain a year.

Models:
    a. Antarctica is a desert because it receives less than 250 millimeters of rain a year.
    b. Like other deserts, Antarctica receives less than 250 millimeters of rain a year.
    c. Because Antarctica receives less than 250 millimeters of rain a year, it is considered to be a desert.

1. The midge is an invertebrate. An invertebrate does not have a backbone.

    a. _____
    b. _____
    c. _____

2. Krill are a vital source of food. Penguins and other animals could not survive without them.

    a. _____
    b. _____
    c. _____

Example: Scientists say that the temperature of the air has been increasing. It has been increasing since 1970.

Models:
    a. Scientists say that since 1970 the temperature of the air has been increasing.
    b. According to scientists, the temperature of the air has been increasing since 1970.
    c. The temperature of the air has been increasing since 1970, say scientists.

3. Scientists say that the number of krill has been declining. This has been happening since the 1970s.

    a. _____
    b. _____
    c. _____

4. Scientists say that it's very lonely in Antarctica. It's especially lonely in the winter.

a. _____

b. _____

c. _____

 Writing

What kinds of plants or crops grow in your native country? What kinds of climates do they grow in? What do people use them for? Make a chart about these plants or crops, and then share it with your classmates.

Name of plant or crop	Climate it's grown in	What it's used for

National Parks

lesson 4

© Payl A. Souders/CORBIS

Before You Read

1. Describe a national park you've visited or heard about.

2. What is the purpose of national parks?

3. Do you think it's important to have national parks? Why or why not?

Context Clues

*The words in **bold** print below are from this lesson. Use context clues to guess what each word means.*

1. One goal of the park system was to preserve and protect unique natural landscapes and wildlife **habitats**.

2. With no one **assigned** to protect the area, vandalism by **curious** visitors became a problem.

3. During the summer, the most popular parks are **crowded** and noisy.

4. These parks contain the most **massive** trees on Earth and the tallest mountain in the continental United States.

4   National Parks

For centuries, Native Americans living in what is now the United States and Canada lived close to nature, using only what they needed from the natural environment in order to survive. But when Europeans arrived on the
5   continent, they saw an **abundance** of materials that they could use and sell. They cut down the forests, killed animals for sport, and used farming methods that allowed the wind and rain to erode the soil. To many of the new settlers, it must have seemed that there was an
10   endless supply of forests, animals, and land.

By the 1870s, settlers were moving west in astonishing numbers. It was at this time that a small group of people became concerned about protecting the **magnificent** scenery and abundant wildlife in an area
15   that is now part of the states of Wyoming, Montana, and Idaho. This part of the country had geysers, hot springs, and waterfalls; there were also snow-covered mountains, clear lakes, and huge trees. The group of concerned **citizens** worried that unless these natural
20   wonders were protected by the government, their

great supply (of something)

descendants would never have a chance to see them. In 1872, they **convinced** the U.S. government to make the area into a national park. Called Yellowstone National Park, it was the country's first national park.

persuaded

25　When Yellowstone National Park was created, no one gave much thought to how the park would be managed, who would actually protect it, and where the money to take care of it would come from. In fact, during the park's first few years, no money at all was
30　provided to take care of it. And with no one **assigned** to protect the area, vandalism by **curious** visitors and the killing of wildlife within the park's boundary became serious problems. Finally, in 1883, the government asked the U.S. Army to protect the park, and for the
35　next 30 years, it remained under the army's control. In the final years of the 19th century, more national parks were established, hunting was banned in the parks, and a few roads were built through the parks.

　　Realizing that the national parks needed to be
40　managed and protected, the U.S. government created the National Park System in 1912. The goal of the park system was to create and manage parks that would preserve and protect unique natural landscapes, wildlife **habitats**, and sites of historic or
45　cultural significance.

　　Today, the U.S. National Park System is made up of 375 parks, covering more than 300,000 square kilometers of land. The parks can be used for camping, hiking, fishing and boating. Scientists, **naturalists**, and
50　historians provide information, give talks, and lead guided walks. Unfortunately, the immense popularity of the parks could well be their **undoing**. During the summer, the most popular parks are **crowded** and noisy. The greatest danger to the national parks,

downfall; destruction

55　however, comes from the areas surrounding them. The parks are threatened by pollution from power plants, diversion of water for development, and **urban** development. Today, all of the 375 national parks are being degraded because of overuse and damage to their

related to a city

60　**ecosystems**.

ecological units in nature

Below is a list of some of the most threatened national parks.

Acadia National Park, Maine

With more than 180 square kilometers of rugged
65 Atlantic **shoreline**, 26 mountain peaks, mixed forest,
lakes, islands, and abundant wildlife, Acadia is plagued
by ozone pollution, degraded scenic vistas, acid
deposition, and mercury deposition.

Everglades National Park, Florida

70 Everglades is North America's only subtropical
preserve and the only place on Earth where alligators
and crocodiles coexist. Sadly, southern Florida **registers**
the highest mercury deposition levels anywhere in
America.

75 ### Glacier National Park, Montana

Glacier boasts more than 1,000 kilometers of trails
and hundreds of structures listed on the National
Register of Historic Places. The park's temperature has
risen **dramatically** in the past century and its glaciers
80 have **retreated**—developments that scientists attribute
in part to global warming.

Great Smoky Mountains National Park, North Carolina and Tennessee

The world's salamander capital is the nation's most
85 visited national park. It is also one of the country's
haziest parks. Ozone levels here are harmful both to
plants and to people.

Mammoth Cave National Park, Kentucky

Containing the most extensive known cave system
90 in the world, Mammoth Cave also boasts one of the
most biologically diverse rivers in North America. This
is another one of the country's haziest, most ozone-
polluted parks. Mercury threatens seven endangered
species here.

coastline

laying down
through natural
processes; noun
form of *deposit*

95 *Sequoia and Kings Canyon National Parks, California*
These parks contain the most **massive** trees on Earth
and the tallest mountain in the continental United
States. However, **pesticides** may be linked to a decline

chemicals used to
kill pests

in wildlife in the parks, and the parks' plants are being
100 damaged by ozone.

Shenandoah National Park, Virginia
Shenandoah represents one of America's most
diverse botanical reserves and **hosts** approximately
1,400 known plant species. Acid rain pollutes park
105 streams and has reduced the acid-neutralizing **capacity**
of **sensitive** watersheds.

ability to hold or
store

easily damaged

From http://www.npca.org/across_the_nation/visitor_experience/
code_red/fact_sheets/default.asp. Adapted with permission from the
National Parks Conservation Association.

a Vocabulary

abundance	magnificent	citizens	convince
assigned	curious	habitats	naturalists
undoing	crowded	urban	ecosystem

1. It takes the best materials and a lot of work to build a
   _____ house.

2. It's difficult to move in a _____ room.

3. Urban development is destroying the _____ of many kinds
   of animals.

4. There is an _____ of krill in the water around Antarctica.

5. Only _____ of the country can vote in an election.

6. If the plants in an _____ die, this will affect the other living
   things there.

7. Everyone has an _____ seat on an airplane.

8. Allowing animals to graze was the land's _____. Before
   long, nothing could grow there.

9. If you are _____ about ecosystems, you should try to learn
   more about them.

10. It doesn't make sense to own a car if you live in an _____ area.

11. Many _____ are opposed to drilling in wildlife areas.

12. She had to _____ the group that her plan was the best one.

b Vocabulary

shoreline	deposits	registered	dramatic
hazy	massive	pesticides	capacity
sensitive	host	urban	retreated

1. They tried to protect the most _____ areas in the state by banning motorized vehicles.

2. On a _____ day, it's difficult to see the mountains in the distance.

3. If you dig down into the earth, you will find mineral _____.

4. As the _____ of the party, he made sure that all his guests had enough to eat and drink.

5. You can often find shells and seaweed on the _____.

6. The thermometer _____ an unimaginable −50°F.

7. A temperature increase of 30°F in one hour is a _____ change.

8. My car has a _____ of just four people.

9. The pyramids are _____ structures.

10. Many _____ are dangerous to humans.

11. The wolves _____ when they saw the campfire.

c Vocabulary Review: Odd One Out

Circle the word that doesn't fit in each group.

1. disaster, catastrophe, territory, emergency
2. infertile, degraded, lush, contaminated
3. preserve, appoint, protect, save
4. cheat, murder, exploit, ponder
5. reliable, cooperative, foolhardy, responsible
6. designate, carve, decorate, weave

7. budget, referee, judge, witness
8. arrogant, abusive, respected, combative

d Comprehension Check: Multiple Choice

Circle the letter of the best answer.

1. Unlike Native Americans, many of the new settlers to North America
   _____.
   a. tried to set up national parks
   b. used the land wisely
   c. cut down the forests

2. The first national park in the United States _____.
   a. had geysers and hot springs
   b. became a park in the 18th century
   c. was in California

3. The first national park _____.
   a. didn't have any visitors
   b. wasn't protected
   c. wasn't vandalized

4. The government asked _____ to protect the park.
   a. a group of citizens
   b. curious visitors
   c. the U.S. Army

5. The National Park System protects _____.
   a. only natural areas
   b. more than just natural areas
   c. hunters

6. _____ is banned in some parks.
   a. Hunting
   b. Fishing
   c. Camping

7. Many of the national parks are being degraded in part because of _____.
   a. the abundance of wildlife
   b. the lack of visitors
   c. urban development

8. Sequoia and Kings Canyon National Parks are famous for _____.
   a. their enormous trees
   b. their cave system
   c. their glaciers

e Comprehension Questions

1. How did the European settlers and the Native Americans use the land differently?
2. Where is Yellowstone National Park?
3. Who was responsible for creating Yellowstone National Park?
4. What problems did Yellowstone National Park have in its early years?
5. What is the purpose of the National Park System?
6. How are national parks being threatened today?
7. What types of pollution are affecting the parks?
8. Which of the parks listed on pages 136–137 sounds the most interesting to you? Why?

f Reading Strategy: Identifying Facts and Opinions

Identify each statement below as a fact or an opinion. Write **Fact** *or* **Opinion** *on the line.*

_____ 1. To the early settlers in North America, it must have seemed that there was an endless supply of forests.

_____ 2. Yellowstone National Park has magnificent scenery.

_____ 3. Yellowstone National Park was the country's first national park.

_____ 4. Unfortunately, the immense popularity of national parks could well be their undoing.

_____ 5. It is sad that mercury levels are high in southern Florida.

_____ 6. There are more than 1,000 trails in Glacier National Park.

_____ 7. The most massive tree on Earth is in California.

_____ 8. Pesticides may be linked to a decline in wildlife.

g Vocabulary Expansion: Word Forms

Look at the chart below and circle the suffix that was added to form each noun. Choose the correct form of the word to complete each question, and then answer the questions.

	Verb	Noun
1.	assign	assignment
2.	manage	management
3.	establish	establishment
4.	protect	protection
5.	create	creation
6.	astonish	astonishment
7.	arrive	arrival
8.	inform	information
9.	pollute	pollution
10.	divert	diversion

1. Do you think teachers should _____ homework over the weekend?

2. Would you want to be in charge of the _____ of a large company?

3. Do you think that the _____ of nationals parks is a good idea?

4. What would happen to the parks if they didn't have _____?

5. Do you think that the _____ of international parks is a good idea?

6. How does a person's face show _____?

7. Do you think the time will _____ when the national parks are too polluted to use?

8. What is a good source of _____ about air pollution?

9. Is it against the law to _____ the air and water?

10. How can the _____ of water endanger the land?

h Grammar Review: Transition Words

Use the correct transition word to complete each sentence below.

    however   for example   finally

1. Every year, thousands of tourists visit the area to see the magnificent scenery. _____, it's usually so hazy that they can't see anything in the distance.

2. They worked for years to convince the government to turn the area into a park. _____, in 1872, they got their wish.

3. Many of the national parks are plagued by ozone pollution. _____, Mammoth Cave National Park has an extremely high level of ozone.

4. Acadia National Park has a beautiful shoreline and abundant wildlife. _____, in the summer, air pollution is a serious problem.

5. Some of the national parks include sites of historic importance. _____, a site of an important Civil War battle is part of one national park.

i Sentence Combining

Read the example and the model combinations below. Then rewrite sentences 1 and 2 following the models.

Example: The U.S. government realized that the parks needed protection. For this reason, it created the National Park System.

Models: a. Because the parks needed protection, the U.S. government created the National Park System.
   b. Realizing that the parks needed protection, the U.S. government created the National Park System.
   c. When the U.S. government realized that the parks needed protection, it created the National Park System.

1. The U.S. government realized that the park was being vandalized. For this reason, it asked the U.S. Army to protect the park.

    a. _____

    b. _____

    c. _____

142

2. The citizens feared that the magnificent scenery would be destroyed. To stop this from happening, they asked the government to turn the area into a national park.

a. _____

b. _____

c. _____

j Writing

Imagine that you are visiting a national park. Write a short note describing what you see and hear. Include both facts and opinions in your description.

143

Video Highlights

a Before You Watch

1. Think back to what you've read about U.S. national parks, and answer the questions.

   a. Why were national parks formed?

   b. What threatened Yellowstone National Park when it was first designated a national park?

   c. What is the goal of the National Park Service?

   d. What is threatening the parks now?

2. Read the following quote from the video. Guess the meaning of the underlined words.

   "A <u>conservation</u> group says many of those parks continue to be in <u>jeopardy</u> from everyday threats."

3. You are going to watch a video about other national parks. Discuss in pairs what you think you will see, using some of the following words:

vegetation	secluded	preserve	lush
wilderness	eroded	protection	pollution
magnificent	habitats	urban	threats
shoreline	massive		

b As You Watch

1. Watch the video. What is the bad news about U.S. national parks? What is the good news?

2. Match each national park with the threat it faces.

   a. Florida's Biscayne National Park   _____ development

   b. Great Smoky Mountains National Park   _____ under-funding

   c. The Underground Railroad network   _____ air pollution

C   After You Watch

1. Form groups to answer the following questions.

   a. Which national park would you most like to visit? Why?

   b. What surprised you most about the video?

   c. Do you feel that the problems national parks face are important? Why or why not?

   d. How could the national parks be better protected? How can ordinary people help?

2. The conservationist in the video says that it is the responsibility of the U.S. Congress to protect national parks. Working in a group, imagine that you are all conservationists. How can you convince Congress to spend more money on the parks? Complete the chart, and then present your ideas to the class.

If . . .	then . . .
If we clean up the parks,	then more tourists will come.

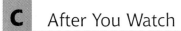 145

Video Highlights

Activity Page

Crossword Puzzle

Across

4. Companies are harvesting krill in Antarctica for _____ uses.
9. Animals are in danger of becoming extinct when their natural _____ is destroyed.
11. setting, where something happens
12. Many cities in the United States have passed legislation to _____ smoking in public places.
13. This bus is too _____. Let's wait for the next one.
14. an unexplored area
15. Hawaii has more _____ diversity than any other state in the United States because people from many countries settled there.
16. huge, massive
17. _____ is one natural cause of desertification.

Down

1. Running a marathon is an amazing _____ of endurance.
2. Many _____ visit Florence every year to see the museums and architecture.
3. Chemical _____ get rid of insects but can be harmful to crops.
5. Someone who asks a lot of questions is _____.
6. Kelly is a _____ of California. She was born in Orange County.
7. grand, majestic
8. land that has water on three sides
10. Disadvantages to living in _____ areas include traffic and pollution.
12. Poor time management skills can be a _____ to completing work on time.

Learning About Word Stress

Your dictionary includes information on which syllables in a word are stressed, or spoken with force or emphasis. The *primary stress* indicates the syllable that should receive the heaviest stress. Some words have a *secondary stress*, which indicates the syllable that should receive the next heaviest stress.

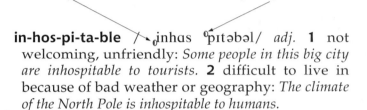

secondary stress   primary stress

in-hos-pi-ta-ble /ˌɪnhɑsˈpɪtəbəl/ *adj.* **1** not welcoming, unfriendly: *Some people in this big city are inhospitable to tourists.* **2** difficult to live in because of bad weather or geography: *The climate of the North Pole is inhospitable to humans.*

1. Look at the words below. Double underline the primary stress. Underline the secondary stress.

   Example: i̱nhospi̱table

uninhabitable	lush
artificial	barren
vulnerable	static
hazy	commercial
colossal	abundant

2. Write each of the above words in the proper column of the chart below, depending on whether its meaning is generally positive or negative or can be either.

ADJECTIVES DESCRIBING PLACES

Positive	Can be positive or negative	Negative
lush		*barren*

Science and Technology

unit
4

I was taught that the way of [scientific]
progress is neither swift nor easy.
—Marie Curie

© Mike Miller/Photo Researchers,Inc.

Satellites

© Rob Matheson/CORBIS

Before You Read

1. What is the definition of a satellite?

2. What are satellites used for?

3. Which country put the first satellite in space?

Context Clues

*The words in **bold** print below are from this lesson. Use context clues to guess what each word means.*

1. Satellites are bodies that travel around a planet. Our Moon is a satellite because it **orbits** the Earth.

2. Some satellites orbit at very high **altitudes** of more than 32,000 kilometers from Earth.

3. Weather satellites have to travel very fast to prevent **gravity** from pulling them back to Earth.

4. Communication satellites have a **lifespan** of 12 to 13 years.

5. Computers on ships and planes can use satellites to **calculate** their position.

1   Satellites

In **astronomy**, satellites are defined as bodies that travel around a planet. Our Moon is a satellite because it **orbits** the Earth. In addition to these natural satellites, there are many human-made satellites **revolving**
5 around the Earth and other planets in our solar system. Some of these satellites orbit at very high **altitudes** of more than 32,000 kilometers from Earth, while others stay close to Earth at altitudes of about 250 kilometers. Each human-made satellite sent into space has a special
10 mission, or purpose, based on the kind of satellite it is. The six major kinds of human-made satellites in space are weather satellites, scientific research satellites, Earth observation satellites, communication satellites, **navigation** satellites, and **military** satellites.
15   Weather satellites help scientists **monitor** the weather patterns on Earth. Information from weather satellites is **invaluable** for making weather forecasts and warning of **potentially** dangerous weather conditions such as hurricanes and tornadoes. Weather satellites travel in
20 what is called low earth orbit (LEO). That means they travel between 320 and 800 kilometers above the Earth. A satellite at this altitude can get detailed pictures of our planet, but it has to travel very fast to prevent **gravity** from pulling it back to Earth. Some of these satellites
25 travel as fast as 27,000 kilometers per hour, orbiting the Earth in just 90 minutes.

    Scientific research satellites travel in space collecting information and conducting experiments to help us better understand the solar system. For example, a
30 satellite called *SOHO* is studying the atmosphere, surface, and internal activity of the Sun. Satellites can serve as unique research laboratories. For example, it's possible to grow high-quality human protein crystals and **tissue** cultures inside a space station because
35 gravity is so low (almost zero). Without the pressure of gravity, the crystals can grow equally in all directions.

---

the science of outer space

distances above sea level

directional guidance for ships and airplanes
armed forces
observe over time
extremely valuable
possibly

152

Deciphering the protein **codes** of these crystals may help in the development of new medicines to combat diabetes, cancer, and other diseases. The tissue cultures may also be used to test new cancer treatments.

figuring out the meaning of; interpreting

Earth observation satellites are used to observe rain forests, water supplies, and other natural resources and to monitor environmental problems such as pollution and deforestation. These satellites are important because they can help control the spread of disease in crops and forests. They can also **detect** fires and floods before they become too big.

find; discover

We use communication satellites for voice, **data**, and television communications around the world. These satellites serve as relay stations, receiving information from one place and sending it on to another place. Most communication satellites stay at a high altitude of about 35,000 kilometers above the Earth. Because of their speed and the size of their orbit, these satellites revolve around in 24 hours. Because the rate at which they travel is the same as the rate of **rotation** of the Earth, the satellites remain over the same place on the Earth's surface. This area on Earth is called the satellite's footprint. If a satellite's footprint covered Africa, for example, a person would use this satellite when communicating with other people in Africa. When someone in Africa wanted to communicate with someone in a different footprint, the message would be relayed using more than one satellite. Today, there are roughly 100 communication satellites orbiting the Earth, each with a **lifespan** of 12 to 13 years. At any one time, a large communication satellite can carry more than 100,000 telephone calls and several television signals.

detailed bits of information

turning on an axis or around a center

Navigation satellites help guide ships at sea and airplanes in the sky. Computers on the ships and planes can **calculate** their position using the information they receive from satellites. Many cars in the 21st century have a global position system, or GPS. A GPS is so **versatile** it can navigate a car around a city block or across an entire country.

capable of doing many things

Lesson 1: Satellites

Military satellites are weather, communication, and observation satellites used for military purposes. Some military satellites are called "spy satellites" because they monitor the activities of other countries and send the

80 information back to their ground stations. These satellites can take extraordinarily detailed pictures of things on the ground, which makes them a powerful tool for the military. For example, they can provide information on the position of ships and aircraft as well

85 as the movement of troops on the ground. Military satellites are also used to ensure safe communications between ships, aircraft, and ground stations. In addition to taking photographs, military satellites have also been used in modern warfare to direct missiles and destroy

90 specific targets.

Satellites are able to stay up in space because they move fast and because the Earth's gravity keeps them there. Imagine tying an object to the end of a long string and spinning it around in the air. The object will remain

95 **in motion** as long as it is moving fast and the string   moving
remains connected. If you stop or cut the string, the object will fall. This is how satellites work. Sometimes they have problems and need to be **repaired**. While this   fixed
can usually be done from Earth by computers, it may be

100 necessary for people to go into space to repair them. If they cannot be repaired, they are simply **disabled** and   made unable to
left to float in space forever. This is what is called   function
"space junk."

It was roughly 50 years ago that the former Soviet

105 Union sent the first human-made satellite into orbit. The football-sized satellite was **appropriately** named   suitably; properly;
Sputnik, which means "satellite" in Russian. *Sputnik 2*   correctly
went up one month later carrying a dog named Laika, the first animal to go into space. Since that time,

110 hundreds of satellites have been sent into orbit around the Earth and other planets in the solar system with the goal of collecting valuable information for people on Earth.

154

a Vocabulary

astronomy	orbit	revolve	altitude
navigation	military	monitor	invaluable
potential	gravity	decipher	code

1. How many moons _____ the planet Jupiter?
2. In the past, ships used the stars for _____.
3. Without _____, we wouldn't be able to stay on the ground.
4. The study of objects in space is called _____.
5. How long does it take for the Earth to _____ around the Sun?
6. When the two countries couldn't negotiate a treaty, the _____ took over.
7. The message was written in _____, and no one could _____ it.
8. I can think of two _____ reasons why the satellite isn't working.
9. At what _____ do people start having trouble breathing?
10. They wouldn't sell the tapestry for any amount of money; it's _____.
11. It's the responsibility of parents to _____ their children's activities.

b Vocabulary

detects	data	rotate	lifespan
calculate	versatile	in motion	repair
disabled	code	appropriate	tissue

1. You can store a lot of _____ in a computer.
2. What's the average _____ of a camel?
3. It's easier to take photographs of things that are standing still than of things that are _____.
4. A smoke alarm _____ smoke before a fire can become large.

155

5. If you want to give them a gift, some flowers would be

                     .

6. The alarm wouldn't stop ringing, so we finally _____ it.

7. A lot of people used to _____ their own cars, but now they pay to have them fixed.

8. The most _____ actors can play many different roles.

9. How long does it take the Earth to _____ once?

10. Do you know how to _____ the area of a triangle?

11. Samples of human _____ are used in research to find treatments for many types of diseases.

C   Vocabulary Review: Antonyms

Match the antonyms.

_____ 1. imperative	a. slow down
_____ 2. succeed	b. clear
_____ 3. accelerate	c. hardy
_____ 4. crowded	d. unnecessary
_____ 5. barren	e. in motion
_____ 6. hazy	f. fertile
_____ 7. massive	g. harvest
_____ 8. sensitive	h. natural
_____ 9. artificial	i. repair
_____ 10. static	j. fail
	k. small
	l. empty

d Comprehension Check: True/False/Not Enough Information

_____ 1. All satellites orbit the Earth.

_____ 2. Weather satellites travel at a lower altitude than communication satellites do.

_____ 3. Weather satellites travel very fast.

_____ 4. The rate at which weather satellites orbit the Earth is the same as the rate at which the Earth rotates.

_____ 5. The satellite *SOHO* orbits the Earth.

_____ 6. The lack of gravity in a satellite makes it difficult to do research.

_____ 7. Observation satellites can help prevent large fires.

_____ 8. There is one primary communication satellite in orbit around the Earth.

_____ 9. Military satellites can take detailed photographs.

_____10. Useless satellites are usually destroyed.

e Comprehension Questions

1. What is the definition of a satellite?
2. What are the six main types of satellites?
3. Why do you think weather satellites travel in low earth orbit?
4. Why do weather satellites have to travel very fast?
5. What is the mission of the satellite *SOHO*?
6. Why are scientists using a space station to grow protein crystals and tissue cultures?
7. What is a satellite's footprint?
8. What are three facts about communication satellites?
9. What are two important missions of military satellites?
10. What is "space junk"?

157

Reading Strategy: Main Ideas and Details

In the chart below, identify the main idea in each paragraph. Then summarize the most important details in your own words.

Paragraph	Main idea	Important details
1 (lines 1–14)	Satellites are bodies that orbit a planet.	Some are natural, and some are human-made. They travel at different altitudes. There are six main kinds: weather, research, Earth observation, communication, navigation, and military.
2 (lines 15–26)		
3 (lines 27–40)		
4 (lines 41–47)		
5 (lines 48–68)		
6 (lines 69–75)		
7 (lines 76–90)		
8 (lines 91–103)		
9 (lines 104–113)		

g Vocabulary Expansion: Word Forms

Choose the right word form for each sentence below.

	Verb	Noun	Adjective	Adverb
1.		astronomy astronomer	astronomical	astronomically
2.	rotate	rotation		
3.	calculate	calculations		
4.	disable	disability	disabled	
5.	communicate	communication communicator	communicative	
6.	detect	detection detector detective		
7.	orbit	orbit	orbital	
8.	navigate	navigation navigator		

1. The government is spending less money on _____ research these days. That's why there are now more unemployed

   _____.

2. The Earth _____ on its axis. It makes one full

   _____ in 24 hours.

3. What instruments do astronomers use to _____ the distance to faraway stars?

4. He was injured at work. Because of his _____, he gets a check every month.

5. Some people are more _____ than others.

6. Dogs can _____ many smells that humans are not aware of.

7. There is a lot of space junk in _____ around Earth.

8. Could you _____ a boat across the ocean without special equipment designed for _____?

Rewrite each sentence below by changing the active verbs to passive verbs and the passive verbs to active verbs.

Example: Earth observation satellites are used to observe the Earth's rain forests.

We use Earth observation satellites to observe the Earth's rain forests.

1. Weather satellites warn 159us of potentially dangerous weather conditions.

   _____

2. Observation satellites can detect fires before they spread.

   _____

3. Navigation satellites guide ships at sea and airplanes in the sky.

   _____

4. Information on the movement of troops on the ground is provided by military satellites.

   _____

5. Satellites in orbit can sometimes be repaired by computers on Earth.

   _____

6. The former Soviet Union sent the first human-made satellite into orbit.

   _____

i   Sentence Combining

Read the example and the model combinations below. Then rewrite sentences 1 and 2 following the models.

Example: Military satellites are used to take photographs of troop movements. They are also used to direct missiles.

Models: a. Military satellites are used to take photographs of troop movements and direct missiles.
b. In addition to taking photographs of troop movements, military satellites are used to direct missiles.
c. Taking photographs of troop movements and directing missiles are two uses of military satellites.

1. Scientific research satellites are used to study the Sun. They are also used to do laboratory experiments.

   a. _____
   b. _____
   c. _____

2. Weather satellites are used to collect information about weather patterns. They can also give warnings of dangerous weather conditions.

   a. _____
   b. _____
   c. _____

j   Writing

The reading in this lesson discussed six types of human-made satellites. Choose something of interest to you that comes in at least three different types. In your writing, give information about each type. Before you start writing, you might want to collect ideas in a chart like the one on page 158.

  161

lesson

2

Comets

© NICK WHITE/Peter Arnold, Inc.

Before You Read

1. What do you know about comets?

2. Have you ever seen a comet in the sky?

3. A long time ago, people were afraid of comets. Why do you think that was?

Context Clues

*The words in **bold** print below are from this lesson. Use context clues to guess what each word means.*

1. These **bizarre** objects seemed to appear suddenly out of nowhere, and they seemed to have no predictable pattern.

2. Some people thought comets were **messengers**, bringing news of disasters to come.

3. Halley **compiled** his data in a book about the location of the stars in the sky.

4. In 2004, the *Stardust* spacecraft flew **within** 236 kilometers of a comet called Wild 2.

5. If we are **fortunate**, comets will provide us with answers to some important questions.

163

2   Comets

If you happen to gaze up in the sky at just the right time in the year 2061, you might get to see one of the most famous comets of all. It's called Halley's Comet, and people get a chance to see it every 76 years when
5 the comet's orbit brings it close to Earth.

Comets are satellites made up **primarily** of ice (both   mainly
water and frozen gases) and dust. All comets orbit the
Sun, but some complete a revolution of the Sun in just a
few years while others need several hundred thousand
10 years. When a comet passes close to the Sun, the ice in
the comet melts and dust **particles** are released. These   very small pieces
dust particles form the comet's famous tail, or "long
hair," which can extend for more than 10 million
kilometers. It should be no surprise that the word *comet*
15 comes from the Greek word *kometes*, which means
"long-haired."

For much of human history, people were terrified of
comets. These **bizarre** objects seemed to appear suddenly   very strange
out of nowhere, and unlike the Sun and stars, they
20 seemed to have no predictable pattern. Some people
thought comets were **messengers**, bringing news of
disasters to come. Comets were blamed for earthquakes,
wars, floods, and an **assortment** of other catastrophes. It
wasn't until late in the 17th century that Sir Isaac Newton
25 discovered that comets orbit the Sun in predictable
patterns, a discovery that helped to **dispel** many people's   get rid of
fear of the long-haired messengers of **doom**.   unhappy ending

Edmond Halley, another famous astronomer, was
born in London, England, in 1656. He studied
30 astronomy at Oxford University until 1676, when he
went off to study the stars and planets of the southern
hemisphere. Later, he **compiled** his data in a book about
the location of the stars in the sky; he was the first
person to map them accurately. Halley also observed
35 the Moon and studied how it affects the ocean tides. He
helped to find a way to measure distances in space. This
measurement system was used by other scientists to

164

learn about the size of our solar system and the
distances of many stars and planets from Earth.

40   Edmond Halley was especially **fond** of studying
comets. He read about comets and observed them in the
sky. He learned about the way they move around the
Sun, each comet following a different path and traveling
at its own speed. Over time, he calculated the orbits of
45 24 comets that he had either read about or seen himself.

    Halley noticed that the paths of a comet seen in 1531
and of a comet seen in 1607 were identical to the path of
a comet he had observed in 1682. He concluded that
these three comets were, in fact, the same comet.
50 Because Halley accurately predicted that the comet
would come again in 1758, it was decided to name the
comet after him. The earliest known reports of Halley's
Comet were actually made over 2,000 years ago by
Chinese astronomers, so we know that it has been
55 orbiting the Sun for more than 2,000 years. Halley's
Comet is one of the brightest comets—bright enough for
people to see without a telescope.

    The orbits of more than 850 comets have now been
calculated. Of these, at least 184 are called **periodic**
60 comets because they orbit the Sun in less than 200 years.
Studying comets may give us information about the
origins and **formation** of the solar system. In 2004, the   beginnings
Stardust spacecraft flew <u>**within**</u> 236 kilometers of a   inside
comet called Wild 2. From this distance, the *Stardust*
65 was able to take extraordinarily detailed photographs of
the comet. Then, in a 12-minute pass through Wild 2's
dust and gas cloud, the *Stardust* mission was able to
collect a spoonful of comet dust to bring back to Earth
for <u>**further**</u> study. Another spacecraft called *Rosetta* is   additional; more
70 expected to actually land on a comet named
Churyumov-Gerasimenko in the year 2014.

    With satellites providing more and more
information, comets will continue to <u>**captivate**</u>   interest greatly
professional and amateur astronomers, as well as the
75 **general** public. And if we are **fortunate**, comets may
soon answer some <u>**fundamental**</u> questions about the   basic; primary
origins of the solar system.

 165

a Vocabulary

primary	particle	messenger	dispel
doomed	periodically	originated	formation
further	fundamentals	fond	fortunate

1. She got a _____ of sand in her eye, and now it hurts.
2. Wouldn't you rather be a _____ of good news than of bad news?
3. Where can you get _____ information about comets?
4. My _____ reason for leaving the job was the long hours.
5. You need to understand the _____ of science before you specialize.
6. He's _____ of cats, but he doesn't like dogs.
7. He thinks he is _____ to die young just because his father did.
8. The _____ of the solar system may never be described accurately.
9. She took a short plane trip to try to _____ her fear of flying.
10. My sister doesn't live very far away so I get to visit her

_____ .

11. She is _____ to have friends who care so much about her.
12. That very tall tree _____ from a tiny seed.

b Vocabulary

bizarre	assortment	compile	within
further	captivating	dispelled	general
fond	origin	primarily	fortunately

1. There is an _____ of drinks on the table. Choose the one you want.
2. This book has a _____ story. I don't think you'll be able to put it down.
3. She likes to _____ a list of things she needs before she goes shopping.

4. You can do many different things with a _____ purpose tool.
5. After his accident, he started doing _____ things like singing on the train and throwing things at people.
6. There was a fire at the school, but _____ no children were there at the time.
7. What is the _____ of the word *comet*?
8. He said he would be here _____ an hour, but it has already been an hour and 20 minutes and he's still not here.
9. Weather satellites are used _____ for collecting information about the weather.
10. He's _____ of all his grandchildren, but I think he likes Sylvia best.
11. By coming to the meeting, the president _____ reports that he was very sick.
12. After they completed the first part of the test, the students needed _____ instruction.

C Vocabulary Review: Definitions

Match the words with their definitions.

_____ 1. livestock
_____ 2. off-limits
_____ 3. fired
_____ 4. adapt
_____ 5. millennia
_____ 6. utopia
_____ 7. drought
_____ 8. commercial
_____ 9. abundant
_____ 10. lifespan

a. baked at a high temperature
b. a perfect place
c. a period of time with very little rain
d. farm animals such as cattle and chickens
e. existing in great amounts
f. something you can't get rid of
g. the number of years something lives
h. bring back to life
i. change in order to survive
j. thousands of years
k. not available; forbidden
l. money-making

 <u>167</u>

d Comprehension Check: Multiple Choice

Circle the letter of the best answer.

1. All comets _____.
   a. orbit the Earth
   b. consist of ice and dust
   c. appear every 76 years

2. When a comet gets close to the Sun, _____.
   a. the dust particles melt
   b. it slows down
   c. the ice melts

3. People used to be afraid of comets because _____.
   a. they didn't appear regularly
   b. they were made of ice and dust
   c. they orbited the Sun

4. People were less afraid of comets after Newton discovered that comets _____.
   a. travel in a regular pattern
   b. orbit the Earth in a pattern
   c. are messengers of doom

5. Edmond Halley was _____.
   a. a French astronomer
   b. ignorant of comets
   c. a compiler of data about comets

6. Halley's Comet appears _____.
   a. every 60 years
   b. periodically
   c. at unexpected times

7. The first report of Halley's Comet was _____.
   a. over 2,000 years ago
   b. in 1531
   c. in 1758

8. Halley's Comet will appear again near Earth in _____.
   a. 2061 and 2102
   b. 2061 and 2127
   c. 2061 and 2137

9. The *Stardust* mission collected ————.
   a. ice from a comet
   b. dust from a comet
   c. photographs of the Sun
10. The satellite *Rosetta* is supposed to ———— the comet

   Churyumov-Gerasimenko.
   a. set down on
   b. destroy
   c. navigate

e Comprehension Questions

1. What are three ways in which all comets are alike?
2. What are three ways in which comets are different from each other?
3. In the past, why were people terrified of comets?
4. In the past, what did people think comets were?
5. What did Sir Isaac Newton discover about comets?
6. What did Edmond Halley learn about comets?
7. Why did Edmond Halley have a comet named after him?
8. What did the *Stardust* mission do to help us learn more about comets?
9. What is the *Rosetta*'s mission?
10. Why do you think so many people are captivated by comets?

Reading Strategy: Identifying Cause and Effect

When you read, it's important to notice the cause and effect relationship between ideas in the text.

Match each cause on the left to an effect on the right. Write the number of the cause on the line.

Cause

1. People didn't understand what comets were.
2. A comet moves close to the Sun.
3. Some comets are very bright.
4. The satellite flew within 236 kilometers of the comet.
5. The satellite flew through the comet's tail.

Effect

_____ The Sun melts the ice in the comet.

_____ It was able to take detailed photographs.

_____ It was able to collect dust particles.

___1___ They were afraid of comets.

_____ You can see them without a telescope.

_____ They reported its appearance over 2,000 years ago.

 Vocabulary Expansion: Collocations

We often use certain nouns and verbs together. For example, the verb *dispel* means "to cause something to go away," but only certain things can be *dispelled*. You might talk about dispelling someone's shyness, but you probably wouldn't talk about dispelling a wild animal.

Match the verbs and nouns that you can use together. Write the number of one or more verbs next to each noun.

Verbs

1. dispel
2. combat
3. compile
4. divert
5. monitor
6. harvest
7. commit
8. applaud

Nouns

_____ a. facts
_____ b. someone's attention
_____ c. crops
_____ d. a crime
_____ e. someone's fear
_____ f. the water in a river
_____ g. someone's performance
_____ h. vandalism
_____ i. a disease
_____ j. statistics
_____ k. the ship's movements
_____ l. someone's belief
_____ m. a child's temperature

 Grammar Review: Compound Nouns

The words *space station* and *research satellite* are called compound nouns because they are formed by putting two nouns together.

Use the nouns below to form 10 compound nouns. Write your compound nouns on the lines given.

military   barrier   research
solar   navigation   management
system   code   data
emergency   satellite   catastrophe
facility   treaty

1. _____
2. _____
3. _____
4. _____
5. _____

6. _____
7. _____
8. _____
9. _____
10. _____

i Sentence Combining

Read the example and the model combinations below. Then rewrite sentences 1 to 3 following the models.

Example: Halley correctly predicted that the comet would appear again in 1758. For this reason, it was decided to name the comet after him.

Models: a. Because Halley correctly predicted that the comet would appear again in 1758, it was decided to name the comet after him.
   b. It was decided to name the comet after Halley because he correctly predicted that it would appear again in 1758.
   c. The reason the comet was named after Halley was that he correctly predicted that it would appear again in 1758.

1. Newton explained that comets moved in predictable patterns. For this reason, people weren't so afraid when they saw a comet in the sky.

   a. _____

   b. _____

   c. _____

2. Halley's Comet is an extremely bright comet. For this reason, you don't have to have a telescope to see it.

   a. _____

   b. _____

   c. _____

3. Halley spent a long time studying the location of the stars. For this reason, he was able to make an accurate map of the stars.

   a. _____

   b. _____

   c. _____

j Writing

Have you ever thought about traveling in space? Imagine that you are exploring the solar system. Use your imagination to write a description of your trip.

Motor Vehicles: The Pros and Cons

lesson 3

© Adamsmith/Getty Images

Before You Read

1. What are some positive effects of automobiles?

2. What are some negative effects of automobiles?

3. What do you think the future of the automobile is?

173

Context Clues

*The words in **bold** print below are from this lesson. Use context clues to guess what each word means.*

1. **In spite of** their advantages, motor vehicles have many critics because of their harmful effects.

2. At **peak** traffic periods in Los Angeles, it can take three hours to drive only 32 kilometers.

3. Two-thirds of its downtown area is **devoted** to roads, parking lots, gas stations, and other automobile-related uses.

4. Automobiles and highways have provided almost unlimited **mobility** to people in the United States.

3   Motor Vehicles: The Pros and Cons

The automobile has many advantages. Above all, it offers people the freedom to go where they want to go, when they want to go there. The basic purpose of a motor vehicle is to get people from point A to point B as
5 cheaply, quickly, and safely as possible. However, to most people, cars are also personal **fantasy** machines   dream; illusion
that serve as **symbols** of power, success, speed, excitement, and adventure.

In addition, much of the world's economy is built on
10 producing motor vehicles and supplying roads, services, and repairs for those vehicles. Half of the world's paychecks and resource use are auto related.

In the United States, one of every six dollars spent and one of every six nonfarm jobs are connected to the
15 automobile or related industries, such as oil, steel, rubber, plastics, automobile services, and highway **construction**. These industries **account for** 20 percent of   explain
the **annual** GNP and provide about 18 percent of all federal taxes. Together, they also are the world's largest
20 **consumer** of energy and raw materials.   users

In spite of their advantages, motor vehicles have many critics because of their harmful effects on human lives and on air, water, land, and wildlife. The automobile may be the most **destructive** machine ever invented.
25 Though we tend to **deny** it, riding in cars is one of the   refuse to admit
most dangerous things we do in our daily lives.

Since 1885, when Karl Benz built the first automobile, almost 18 million people have been killed by motor vehicles. Every year, cars and trucks worldwide kill an
30 average of 250,000 people—as many as were killed in the atomic bomb attacks on Hiroshima and Nagasaki—and injure or permanently disable 10 million more. Half of the world's people will be involved in an auto accident at some time during their lives.

175

35　　By providing almost unlimited **mobility**, automobiles and highways have been the biggest **factor** leading to urban **sprawl** in the United States and other countries with large livable land areas. This **dispersal** of businesses and people from cities has made it
40　increasingly difficult for subways, trolleys, and buses to be economically **feasible alternatives** to private cars.

cause; fact to be considered

outward growth

spreading out in different directions

possible

　　Los Angeles is a global symbol of urban sprawl, built around a vast network of freeways. An estimated one-third of the city's total metropolitan area and two-
45　thirds of its downtown area are **devoted** to roads, parking lots, gas stations, and other automobile-related uses. Each day, its network of streets and freeways is crowded with more than 5 million vehicles, which are responsible for 85 percent of both the air pollution and
50　the noise in this urban area. At **peak** traffic periods, it can take three hours to drive only 32 kilometers.

　　In 1907, the average speed of horse-drawn vehicles through New York city was 18.5 kilometers per hour. Today, cars and trucks with the potential power of 100
55　to 300 horses creep along New York City streets at an average speed of 8 kilometers per hour. In London, average auto speeds are about 13 kilometers per hour, and they are even lower in Paris and in Tokyo, where everyday traffic is called *tsukin jigoku*, or
60　"commuting hell."

　　Streets that used to be for people are now for cars. **Pedestrians** and people riding bicycles in the streets are subjected to noise, pollution, stress, and danger.

people who are walking

　　Motor vehicles are the largest source of air pollution,
65　producing a haze of smog over the world's cities. In the United States, they produce at least 50 percent of the country's air pollution, even though U.S. **emission** standards are as **strict** as any in the world.

something sent out into the air

difficult to obey

　　Worldwide, motor vehicles account for 13 percent of
70　the input of the primary greenhouse gas, carbon dioxide (CO_2), into the atmosphere. In the United States, they account for almost 25 percent of the country's CO_2 emissions (the highest in the world) and 13 percent of the emissions of chlorofluorocarbons, which act as

176

75 greenhouse gases and also **deplete** life-**sustaining** ozone in the stratosphere.

use up; reduce by using too much

keeping in existence; maintaining

Motor vehicle use is also responsible for water pollution from oil spills, gasoline spills, and leakage and dumping of used engine oil, as well as contamination of
80 underground drinking water from leaking underground oil and gasoline storage tanks.

Oil addiction, based mostly on addiction to energy-inefficient gasoline-powered vehicles, also increases the chance of wars, as the United States and other countries
85 **attempt** to protect oil supplies in the oil-rich but **volatile** Middle East. What do you think should be done?

likely to change suddenly; explosive

From *Living in the Environment: Principles, Connections, and Solutions*, 7th edition by G. Tyler Miller © 1992. Reprinted with permission of Brooks/Cole, a division of Thomson Learning: www.thomsonrights.com.

a Vocabulary

fantasy	symbol	construction	account for
annual	consumes	in spite of	deny
mobile	factor	sprawled	disperse

1. The Olympic _____ consists of five rings.
2. My _____ is to sail around the world, but I know it will never happen.
3. The rising cost of gasoline was one _____ in his decision to get rid of his car.
4. Your _____ income is 12 times your monthly income.
5. A large truck _____ gasoline faster than a small car.
6. People keep buying large cars _____ the harmful pollution they create.
7. You don't have to have a car to be _____.
8. No one can walk into this room because the children are _____ on the floor, watching TV.

177

9. How can she _____ causing the accident? I saw her do it.
10. The wind helps to _____ the seeds.
11. _____ jobs are among the most dangerous.
12. I can't _____ the time between 3 p.m. and 4 p.m. today. Maybe I fell asleep.

b Vocabulary

feasible	alternative	devote	peak
pedestrians	emissions	strict	depleted
attempted	volatile	sustain	destructive

1. My boss is a _____ person; it doesn't take much to make him angry.
2. Solar-powered cars are an _____ to gasoline-powered cars.
3. The rules were very _____ when the children were young, but as they got older, the rules were relaxed.
4. The football team gave their _____ performance last weekend. I really don't think they could have done any better.
5. They _____ to drive across the country in a week, but it actually took them longer than that.
6. Much of our air pollution comes from car _____.
7. The runners are going fast, but I don't think they can _____ that speed for long.
8. In some states, you have to stop for _____ who are trying to cross the street.
9. It's not _____ to drive there in 8 hours, but I think you can get there in 10 hours.
10. He can _____ several hours to the project tomorrow, but that's all.
11. The local gasoline supplies were _____. Therefore, they couldn't use their car.
12. Cutting down the trees had a _____ effect on the mountainside.

c Vocabulary Review: Odd One Out

Circle the word that doesn't fit in each group.

1. register, rotate, revolve, orbit
2. doom, disaster, motion, catastrophe
3. deplete, detect, decline, decrease
4. barren, inhospitable, secluded, infertile
5. daring, bold, courageous, curious
6. astronomy, history, erosion, geology
7. incredibly, extremely, dramatically, appropriately
8. peninsula, pesticides, erosion, drought

d Comprehension Check: True/False/Not Enough Information

_____ 1. The highway construction industry is the world's largest consumer of raw materials.

_____ 2. One of the harmful effects of automobiles is air pollution.

_____ 3. Riding in cars is the most dangerous thing we do.

_____ 4. More than 10 million people have been killed in motor vehicle accidents.

_____ 5. The first car was built in Germany in 1885.

_____ 6. Fifty percent of the people in the world will be in a motor vehicle accident at some time in their lives.

_____ 7. When a city is spread out over a large area, it's difficult to provide good public transportation for the people who live there.

_____ 8. In Los Angeles, it can take three hours to drive 32 kilometers.

_____ 9. Vehicles in New York City travel more slowly now than they did in 1907.

_____10. The United States has the highest carbon dioxide emissions of any country in the world.

Comprehension Questions

1. What are some advantages of cars?
2. If people stopped using cars, what effect would this have on the economy?
3. How many people are killed each year in car and truck accidents?
4. What percentage of the world's people will be involved in at least one car or truck accident during their lives?
5. What is the connection between urban sprawl and cars?
6. Why isn't public transportation a feasible alternative to cars in the United States?
7. If there were suddenly no fuel for cars, what would Los Angeles be like?
8. How has traveling by car in New York City changed since 1907?
9. What role do cars play in polluting the air?
10. What are some other disadvantages of cars?

 Reading Strategy: Classifying

There are many different ways the ideas in a text can be organized. Organizing by time sequence and organizing by cause and effect are just two of the more common ways. Once you understand how a text is organized, it's easier to take notes and remember what you read.

The ideas in the text on pages 175–177 are organized by advantages and disadvantages. Use the T-chart below to make notes on the ideas in the text.

Advantages	Disadvantages

180

Vocabulary Expansion: Suffixes

You can add the suffix *-ly* or *-ally* to many adjectives to form an adverb.

Choose the correct form of the word in the chart to complete each question below. Then answer the questions.

	Adjective	Adverb
1.	annual	annually
2.	symbolic	symbolically
3.	alternative	alternatively
4.	strict	strictly
5.	persistent	persistently
6.	curious	curiously
7.	former	formerly
8.	unimaginable	unimaginably

1. What is one thing you do _____?
2. How can you represent the word *love* _____?
3. What is one _____ plan to putting your money in a bank?
4. Do you think city streets should be _____ for pedestrians?
5. What is one thing you have to practice _____ in order to become good at it?
6. What is one place on Earth that you are _____ about?
7. Where did you _____ go to school?
8. What is one thing that it would be _____ for you to do?

h Grammar Review: Noun Substitutes

*Read each sentence or pair of sentences and study the pronoun in **bold** print. Circle the noun or noun phrase that each pronoun replaces.*

1. The automobile has many advantages. Above all, **it** offers people freedom.
2. In spite of **their** advantages, motor vehicles have many critics because of their harmful effects on human lives and on air, water, land, and wildlife.
3. Though we tend to deny **it**, riding in cars is one of the most dangerous things we do in our daily lives.
4. An estimated one-third of the city's total metropolitan area and two-thirds of **its** downtown area are devoted to roads, parking lots, gas stations, and other automobile-related uses.
5. In London, average auto speeds are about 13 kilometers per hour, and **they** are even lower in Paris.
6. Motor vehicles are the largest source of air pollution, producing a haze of smog over the world's cities. In the United States, **they** produce at least 50 percent of the country's air pollution, even though U.S. emission standards are as strict as any in the world.
7. Worldwide, motor vehicles account for 13 percent of the input of the primary greenhouse gas, carbon dioxide (CO_2), into the atmosphere. In the United States, **they** account for almost 25 percent of the country's CO_2 emissions.

i Sentence Combining

Read the example and the model combinations below. Then rewrite sentences 1 and 2 following the models.

Example: Los Angeles is a global symbol of urban sprawl. It is built around a vast network of freeways.

Models: a. Los Angeles, which is built around a vast network of freeways, is a global symbol of urban sprawl.
  b. Los Angeles is a global symbol of urban sprawl, built around a vast network of freeways.
  c. Built around a vast network of freeways, Los Angeles is a global symbol of urban sprawl.

182

1. Automobile-related businesses make up a huge industrial complex. They are responsible for 20 percent of the annual GNP.

    a. _____

    b. _____

    c. _____

2. Motor vehicles are harmful to the environment. They are responsible for 25 percent of U.S. carbon dioxide emissions.

    a. _____

    b. _____

    c. _____

j Writing

Think of different ways to complete this title: *The Advantages and Disadvantages of* _____. Choose one idea, and explain its advantage and disadvantages. Later, share your writing with a classmate.

Sample titles
The Advantages and Disadvantages of Reading the Newspaper
The Advantages and Disadvantages of Living in a Foreign Country
The Advantages and Disadvantages of Having a Job You Hate
The Advantages and Disadvantages of Being Short

New Plants

lesson

4

© JOERG BOETHLING/Peter Arnold, Inc.

Before You Read

1. What are some of the most common foods in your country?

2. What foods available today in your area weren't available 10 years ago?

3. What are some ways we can solve the problem of hunger in the world?

184

Unit 4: Science and Technology

Context Clues

*The words in **bold** print below are from this lesson. Use context clues to guess what each word means.*

1. Some types of food are eaten in just a few places, while others, like rice, are eaten **widely**.

2. The cocoyam, which is similar to the potato, can grow in a hot climate **whether** it's wet or dry.

3. Scientists are **optimistic** that people will change the foods they eat, because they have done so in the past.

4. It is now possible to grow a type of Vitamin A–**boosted** rice that has significantly more Vitamin A than other types of rice.

4　New Plants

　　As the population of the world increases, countries
need to produce more and more food. At the same time,
however, deserts are expanding, and millions of people
are building houses on land that used to be farmland.
5　How can we solve a problem that seems to have
no solution?

　　One way to increase the planet's food supply is for
people to start eating different plants. There are more
than 350,000 kinds of plants in the world. Of these,
10　approximately 20,000 are **suitable** for humans to eat.　　　　appropriate
But today, over 50 percent of our food supply comes
from just three kinds of plants: corn, wheat, and rice. In
fact, it is common in developing countries for people to
depend on only one or two plants for their food. A
15　disease or bad weather can destroy these crops, leaving
people with nothing to eat.

　　All people, and especially children, need protein to
grow and to stay healthy. Many kinds of food contain
protein, but some foods are better sources of protein
20　than others. For example, corn, wheat, and rice are only
8 to 14 percent protein. Meat and fish are 20 to 30
percent protein. Soybeans, which are an important food
in China and Japan, are almost 40 percent protein. Other
beans eaten **widely** in Latin America have about the
25　same amount of protein as meat.

　　However, there are other plants that are rich in
protein. People in parts of Papua–New Guinea and in
Southeast Asia eat winged beans, which are over 30
percent protein. The marama bean, as rich in protein as
30　the soybean, grows wild in the Kalahari Desert in
southern Africa.

　　The potato, an important food in Europe and North
America, will not grow in a hot climate. But the
cocoyam, which is similar to the potato, is eaten in Latin
35　America and West Africa. This versatile plant can grow
in a hot climate, and it does not matter **whether** the
climate is wet or dry.

Scientists are now experimenting with crops of buffalo gourds in Mexico and Lebanon. This plant
40 grows wild in Arizona's Sonora Desert, and it could grow in other dry areas as well. The seeds of this plant are up to 35 percent protein.

A few years ago, a new kind of teosinte plant was discovered in the mountains of Mexico. (*Teosinte* is
45 pronounced "tay-oh-SIN-tay.") It is a relative of corn, but it can grow in a wetter climate than corn can. Even more important, teosinte plants can produce crops every year. They do not have to be replanted from seeds as corn does.

50 **Nevertheless**, there may be a problem with "new" plants. Will people be willing to eat them? Food is an important part of our lives, and it is often difficult to change to a new and different kind of food. However, scientists are **optimistic**. They know that 500 years ago
55 Europeans thought they were eating the best food in the world. Then, in the 16th century, a wide assortment of new foods, such as potatoes, tomatoes, pineapple, and chocolate, started arriving by boat from Central and South America. At first most Europeans wouldn't touch
60 these bizarre foods. In fact, many people thought these foods were poisonous. Over time, however, people accepted these foods, and now it's hard to imagine Italian food without tomatoes or a British meal without potatoes. In the 1920s, George Washington Carver
65 started experimenting with the peanut, which is as rich in protein as meat. He developed many ways to use the peanut as food, and today it is eaten all over the world. Perhaps in a few years teosinte and the marama bean will be as widely used as the peanut. And consider the
70 soybean, which is now the most important plant in the United States. Eighty years ago, the soybean wasn't even grown as an industrial crop!

Some people feel strongly that **genetically** engineered food could solve the world's food **crisis**.
75 Humans have been using **selective breeding** for millennia to improve food crops, but genetic engineering provides a way to greatly accelerate the

however; in spite of that

disaster; catastrophe

Lesson 4: New Plants

process and to introduce **traits** from unrelated species. Today, many crops have been genetically **modified** to
80 be resistant to some types of **pests**, while others have been engineered to make them taste better or last longer. Available also are plants that have been genetically **altered** to make them more **nutritious**. **Biotechnology companies** call them "**prescription**"
85 foods because they are supposed to solve health problems. Examples of prescription foods are Vitamin A–**boosted** golden rice and protein-**enhanced** potatoes. Other crops have been modified to make them drought- or salt-resistant, which makes it possible for them to
90 grow in poor soil.

The production of genetically modified (GM) food is highly controversial. Environmentalists worry that these crops could eventually become uncontrollable weeds or that they might breed with wild plants or
95 other crops. Some scientists claim that genetic engineering will actually have a negative **impact** on crop **yields** and soil quality and in the end will just **deprive** more farmers of land on which they could grow their own food.
100 In addition to concerns about how GM crops might affect the environment, there is the question of whether these crops would actually have a positive effect on the global food shortage. Some people have suggested that biotech companies have started promoting GM foods as
105 a solution to the world's food problem in order to change the negative **impression** that many people have of these foods. There are also many people who believe that prescription foods won't help the situation because they do not **address** the real cause of malnutrition,
110 which is **poverty**. According to Daycha Siripatra, who works for the Alternative Agriculture Network in Thailand, "If the poor had land, they would have better diets. The poor don't need Vitamin A. They need Vitamin L; that's Vitamin Land. And they need Vitamin
115 M; that's Vitamin Money. Malnutrition is because of poverty, not [a lack of] technology."

---

characteristics
changed

changed; modified
high in nutrients
businesses using biochemistry to make new medicines, etc.
increased; raised
improved

effect

a feeling about something

deal with

188

a Vocabulary

suitable	widely	whether	nevertheless
optimistic	genetically	selective	breeding
traits	modify	pest	altered

1. Changing the color of her hair really _____ her appearance.

2. We had to _____ our vacation plans when we realized that we had less money than we thought we had.

3. An _____ person sees the positive side of things.

4. A horse with very good _____ will be expensive.

5. Patience is one of my brother's best _____ .

6. They've decided to go to Costa Rica _____ or not their friends are there.

7. Many more students apply to Harvard than are accepted; it's a _____ school.

8. Some diseases are passed _____ from one generation to the next.

9. Poisonous plants are not _____ for human consumption.

10. Genetically engineered food could possibly solve the world's food crisis; _____ , the production of such foods is highly controversial.

11. Some kind of _____ got into their garden and ate the tomatoes.

12. French is spoken _____ in eastern Canada.

189

b Vocabulary

nutritious	prescription	boost	biotechnology companies
enhance	impact	yields	deprived
address	poverty	impression	crisis

1. Children who are _____ of important nutrients may have serious health problems.

2. He refused to _____ his financial problems until finally he was forced to.

3. To buy most medicines, you need a _____ from a doctor.

4. _____ didn't exist 50 years ago.

5. What was your _____ of the speech? Did you like it?

6. My grandfather had a big _____ on my life.

7. Apples are _____; sugar is not.

8. If you can't get up on the horse, I can give you a _____.

9. It's difficult to believe that there can be so much _____ in such a rich country.

10. The loss of a year's food supply was a _____ for the country.

11. Lack of rain can have a tremendous impact on crop _____.

12. What can you put on a potato to _____ the flavor?

190

c Vocabulary Review: Synonyms

Match the synonyms.

_____ 1. annual   a. build

_____ 2. versatile   b. choice

_____ 3. ban   c. fascinate

_____ 4. construct   d. dispel

_____ 5. hazy   e. forbid

_____ 6. alternative   f. collect

_____ 7. captivate   g. volatile

_____ 8. get rid of   h. yearly

_____ 9. compile   i. unclear

_____ 10. feasible   j. many-sided

                              k. within

                              l. possible

d Comprehension Check: Multiple Choice

Circle the letter of the best answer.

1. Roughly half of our food supply comes from _____ kinds of food.
   a. 350,000
   b. 20,000
   c. 3

2. Winged beans are _____.
   a. from Latin America
   b. as rich in protein as soybeans
   c. more than 30 percent protein

3. The potato is _____.
   a. a hot-weather crop
   b. similar to the cocoyam
   c. originally from Europe

4. The cocoyam _____.
   a. can grow in a hot climate
   b. is an important food in North America
   c. doesn't grow in wet climates

5. Unlike corn, the teosinte plant _____.
   a. prefers a dry climate
   b. produces a crop every year
   c. has to be planted every year

6. Scientists are optimistic that people might be willing to eat new foods, because _____.
   a. they already eat roughly 20,000 different kinds of food
   b. they have done it in the past
   c. they like to change what they eat often

7. When Europeans first saw tomatoes, _____.
   a. they wanted to try them immediately
   b. they knew they were safe to eat
   c. they thought they were poisonous

8. Selective breeding _____.
   a. has been taking place for a long time
   b. is a new thing
   c. is impossible

9. Prescription foods are _____.
   a. genetically altered to be more nutritious
   b. enhanced to taste better
   c. modified to grow in any type of soil

10. Some people say that GM food won't solve the food crisis because _____.
    a. it doesn't provide the right nutrients
    b. it doesn't address the real cause
    c. the food crisis is too serious

e Comprehension Questions

1. Roughly how many kinds of plants are there on Earth? How many of those can people safely eat?
2. Why do you think so much of our food supply comes from just three kinds of plants?
3. What foods are high in protein?
4. What information about soybeans does the text on pages 186–188 provide?
5. How is the cocoyam different from the potato?
6. What is the teosinte plant?
7. In the 16th century, how did Europeans react to new foods introduced from Central and South America?
8. What food did George Washington Carver get people to try? How?
9. What are genetically modified foods?
10. Why do some people oppose genetically modified foods?

f Reading Strategy: Identifying Supporting Ideas

Supporting ideas give information to explain a main idea.

For each main idea below, find supporting ideas in the text on pages 186–188. Write the information in the chart.

Main idea	Supporting ideas
Humans make poor use of the plants on Earth.	
It's possible for people to change their eating habits.	
Food can be genetically modified for many different purposes.	
Some people believe that GM crops can be harmful to the environment.	

 <u>193</u>

g Vocabulary Expansion: Word Forms

Choose the right word form for each sentence below.

	Verb	Noun	Adjective	Adverb
1.	select	selection	selective	selectively
2.	prescribe	prescription	prescriptive	
3.	enhance	enhancement	enhanced	
4.	deprive	deprivation	deprived	
5.	alter	alteration	altered	
6.		nutrient	nutritious	nutritiously
7.		optimism	optimistic	optimistically
8.	resist	resistance	resistant	
9.	modify	modification	modified	
10.	promote	promotion	promoted	

1. Do you watch television _____, or do you just watch whatever is on?
2. Doctors can _____ medicine, but nurses can't.
3. Scientists use chemicals to _____ the flavor of many packaged foods.
4. Water _____ will cause crops to do poorly or die.
5. If your pants are too long, you can take them to a tailor for

   _____.
6. Ice cream is less _____ than fresh fruit.
7. I like to be around _____ people because their

   _____ is contagious.
8. Healthy people are more _____ to the flu than unhealthy people.
9. They _____ the plan by removing several buildings.
10. The _____ of cigarette smoking on television is illegal.

h   Grammar Review: Articles

Put an article in each blank if one is necessary.

Nevertheless, there may be (1) _____ problem with "new" plants. Will people be willing to eat them? Food is (2) _____ important part of our lives, and it is often difficult to change to (3) _____ new and different kind of food. However, scientists are optimistic. They know that 500 years ago Europeans thought they were eating (4) _____ best food in the world. Then, in (5) _____ 16th century, a wide assortment of (6) _____ new foods, such as (7) _____ potatoes, tomatoes, pineapple, and chocolate, started arriving by boat from (8) _____ Central and South America. At first, most Europeans wouldn't touch these bizarre foods. In fact, many people thought these foods were poisonous. Over time, however, people accepted these foods, and now it's hard to imagine (9) _____ Italian food without tomatoes or (10) _____ British meal without potatoes. In the 1920s, George Washington Carver started experimenting with (11) _____ peanut, which is as rich in protein as meat. He developed many ways to use (12) _____ peanut as food, and today it is eaten all over the world. Perhaps in (13) _____ few years teosinte and the marama bean will be as widely used as (14) _____ peanut.

i Sentence Combining

Read the example and the model combinations below. Then rewrite sentences 1 to 3 following the models.

Example: Soybeans are an important food in China and Japan. They are almost 40 percent protein.

Models: a. Soybeans, which are an important food in China and Japan, are almost 40 percent protein.
b. Soybeans, an important food in China and Japan, are almost 40 percent protein.
c. An important food in China and Japan, soybeans are almost 40 percent protein.

1. The cocoyam is a plant eaten in West Africa. It is similar to the potato.

   a. _____

   b. _____

   c. _____

2. Tomatoes are an important food in Italian cooking. They were once believed to be poisonous.

   a. _____

   b. _____

   c. _____

3. Vitamin A–boosted golden rice has been genetically modified to be more nutritious. It is a prescription food.

   a. _____

   b. _____

   c. _____

j Writing

What is your opinion of genetically modified food? Write your opinion and give at least three reasons to support your opinion. Later, share your writing with your classmates.

a Before You Watch

1. List what you think are the five most important inventions of all time. In a group, compare your lists. Why did you choose the inventions you did? Is e-mail on your list? Why or why not?

2. You are going to watch a video about the dangers of e-mail. Match the words and expressions with their definitions.

   a. spam

   b. colleagues

   c. slang

   d. stream of consciousness

   e. analyses

   f. speech-like features

   g. the final blow

   h. adage

   _____ characteristics that make some other kind of communication similar to speaking

   _____ a saying that contains truths or helpful information

   _____ thoughts spoken aloud or written as they come to mind, without reflection

   _____ studies done to find facts and solutions to problems

   _____ unwanted e-mail messages that are sent to many people as a type of junk mail

   _____ the last in a line of problems that makes something fail

   _____ co-workers

   _____ informal language; street language

b As You Watch

There is one mistake in each of the quotes below. Watch the video, and correct the mistakes.

1. "When e-mail came on the scene, its promise, like so many other technological innovations, was that it would save money."

2. "It was bad enough when we were just dealing with the telephone."

197

3. "It seems we're writing more and maybe enjoying it less."
4. "Research has shown that actual analyses of the messages of e-mail do document that it does have many speech-like features that we, in fact, in the past, used to associate with conversation."
5. ". . . the use of slang and lots of run-on sentences with '. . .' in between them, almost like a stream of consciousness, instead of carefully formed syntactically beautiful sentences with question marks at the end of them."
6. "If e-mail has given rise to a new form of communication, it may also be the final blow for another form: discussion."
7. ". . . that old adage about waiting before you speak—well, who has time to think when you're communicating?"

C   After You Watch

1. The presenter in the video never states his opinion explicitly. Which statement best summarizes his opinion?

   a. E-mail is an excellent invention, making it easier to communicate.
   b. E-mail has some disadvantages, but overall it makes life better.
   c. E-mail has made it harder, not easier, to communicate well.

2. Think about the video and your own experiences with e-mail. Write some advantages and disadvantages of e-mail in the chart below. Discuss the subject with a classmate.

Advantages of e-mail	Disadvantages of e-mail

Crossword Puzzle

Across

2. _____ is what keeps people's feet on the ground.
4. The code was too difficult to _____.
5. My brother likes to _____ across the sofa so that there is no room for me to sit down.
11. Jim works in an office, but has a _____ about becoming a movie star.
12. a way to describe someone who is always happy
14. Many people believe that problems such as malnutrition are the result of _____.
15. movement
16. reproduce
18. The belief that murder is wrong is _____ to most cultures.
20. For some people, a fast, expensive car is a _____ of power.
21. Driving on the sidewalk is dangerous because you are likely to hit a _____.

Down

1. With family living all around the world, it's rarely _____ to gather everyone together.
3. Their relationship is very _____, as they are always fighting and making up again.
6. The detectives might find more clues with _____ investigation.
7. Dark hair, freckles, and musical talent are all _____ that you might inherit from your parents.
8. Fruits and vegetables are important to a _____ diet.
9. lucky
10. weird, strange
13. A new virus that is difficult to treat could cause an international health _____.
17. Scientists use special machines to _____ invisible gases.
19. Mount Vesuvius brought _____ to the people of Pompeii.

Dictionary Page

Using Prefixes

1. Look up *biotechnology* in the dictionary. Look at other words that begin with *bio-*.

> **bi·o·chem·is·try** /ˌbaɪoʊˈkɛmɪstri/ *n.* [U] the science of the chemistry of living things
>
> **bi·og·ra·phy** /baɪˈɑgrəfi/ *n.* [C;U] **-phies** the history of a person's life: *He read a biography of a baseball hero.* *-n.* **biographer;** *-adj.* **biographical** /ˌbaɪəˈgræfɪkəl/; *-adv.* **biographically.**
>
> **bi·o·tech·no·lo·gy** /baɪoʊtekˈnalədʒi/ *n.* [U] the business of using biochemistry to develop new medicines and other advances to improve health: *Biotechnology develops new drugs to fight cancer and AIDS.*

2. How are the meanings of the words alike? What does the prefix *bio-* mean?
3. Complete the chart, using your dictionary.

Word	Related word(s)	Prefix	Meaning
biotechnology	*biodegradable* *biography* *biology* *bionic*	bio-	*of living things*
polygon		poly-	
geography		geo-	

Health and Well-Being

The first wealth is health.
—Ralph Waldo Emerson

© Spencer Grant/Photo Edit

Up in Smoke

© Dennis MacDonald/Alamy

Before You Read

1. Why do people smoke?

2. What are some of the negative effects of smoking?

3. Do you think people should be permitted to smoke in public places? Why or why not?

Context Clues

*The words in **bold** print below are from this lesson. Use context clues to guess what each word means.*

1. Native Americans used the tobacco plant in different ways. Some people **rubbed** tobacco leaves on their bodies.

2. The use of tobacco in cigarettes didn't become popular until late in the 19th century. Thanks to an effective advertising campaign in the 1880s, cigarette smoking became **widespread**.

3. In the 1960s, the first warning **labels** appeared on cigarette packages.

4. The children of parents who smoke are more likely to develop **respiratory** problems than are children who grow up in a smoke-free environment.

1   Up in Smoke

Five hundred years ago, you wouldn't have seen anyone growing or smoking tobacco in Europe, the Middle East, Africa, or Asia. Today, however, tobacco is grown in roughly 120 countries, and more than 1 billion
5   people around the world smoke tobacco.

Five hundred years ago, the tobacco plant grew only in the Americas. It was used for a <u>**variety**</u> of purposes, and it was highly valued. Many Native Americans believed that the tobacco plant had medicinal properties.
10   They smoked and chewed tobacco and **rubbed** tobacco leaves on their bodies. Some people believed that the leaves of the tobacco plant helped to reduce pain and heal **wounds** and burns. Others thought tobacco leaves could cure toothaches. In many parts of the Americas,
15   smoking tobacco was also an important part of religious <u>**rites**</u> and ceremonies. People believed that tobacco made it possible to communicate with the spirits.

assortment; range

acts performed in a particular way determined by custom

203

When the first Spanish explorers arrived in the Americas late in the 15th century, they saw Native
20 Americans "smoke drinking," as they called smoking, and they eagerly tried it. When the first Portuguese explorers arrived in the Americas, they **encountered**   met
Native Americans who used tobacco as snuff rather than smoking it. Snuff is **basically** finely ground tobacco,
25 which is **inhaled** through the nose. The Portuguese   breathed in
explorers picked up the snuff habit and exported it to Portugal and much of the rest of the world. The Portuguese were also the first people to **cultivate** the   grow
tobacco plant outside of the Americas. The French
30 ambassador to Portugal, Jean Nicot de Villemain, called tobacco a cure-all for many illnesses, and in 1560 he sent samples of the tobacco plant to France, where it was given the name *Nicotiana* in his **honor**.   recognition with appreciation

Tobacco was probably taken to England by Spanish
35 and English explorers, who had learned to smoke it in pipes rather than use it as snuff. People in England were at first frightened by the sight of smoke coming out of a person's mouth. The first smokers there were followed and stared at. Before long, however, pipe smoking was a
40 popular activity.

Not everyone in Europe and Asia welcomed the arrival of tobacco and the smoking habit. In Russia, possession of tobacco was forbidden. In Turkey and India, smokers faced the death penalty. The Catholic
45 Pope banned its use in the early 1600s. Both the use and the cultivation of tobacco were banned in Japan in 1609 and in China in 1612. Despite this, smoking gained in popularity. The **failure** of the bans was due in large part to the fact that governments could make money from
50 the sale of tobacco. For example, King James I of England strongly opposed the use of tobacco, but he often needed money, and **taxing** imported tobacco was an easy way for him to get it.

The use of tobacco in cigarettes didn't become
55 popular until late in the 19th century. Thanks to an effective advertising campaign in the 1880s, cigarette

204

smoking became **widespread**. Back then, most people thought that cigarettes helped to relieve tension; they didn't believe that cigarettes were harmful to a person's
60 health. In the 20th century, however, doctors began seeing an increasing number of cases of **lung** cancer, and in 1950 researchers in England reported the first evidence showing a link between smoking and lung cancer. Fourteen years later, in 1964, the U.S. Surgeon
65 General announced that smoking causes lung cancer. Soon after that, the first warning **labels** appeared on cigarette packages, and cigarette advertisements were banned from television and radio in England and the United States. The tobacco industry responded by
70 paying filmmakers to show actors and actresses smoking in their movies. Fearing that the health warnings would encourage people to stop smoking, cigarette makers also increased the amount of nicotine in cigarettes to make them more addictive.

75   Today, we know that there are about 4,000 different chemicals in the smoke of an average cigarette. Some of these chemicals are **toxic**, and at least 60 of them cause   **poisonous** cancer. Nicotine, for example, is highly addictive and poisonous. We know that smoking is the **leading** cause   **primary; main**
80 of lung diseases, and it has also been linked to heart disease and other kinds of cancer. There is evidence that smokers have more trouble healing after surgery, and they are at greater risk for **post-op** **complications**.   **after an operation; after surgery**
    In addition to harming smokers, cigarette smoke can   **problems; difficulties**
85 have a negative effect on the health of nonsmokers **occupying** the same environment. Researchers think   **being in** that each year **secondhand** smoke may be responsible   **used before by someone else** for about 3,000 lung cancer deaths and 35,000 cases of heart disease among nonsmoking adults. And not only
90 adults are affected by inhaling secondhand smoke. The children of parents who smoke are more likely to develop **respiratory** problems than are children who grow up in a smoke-free environment.
    While people have been opposed to smoking as far
95 back as the 1600s, there is now an increasing amount of

Lesson 1: Up in Smoke

pressure on smokers to kick the habit. In 1993, the state
of Vermont in the United States banned smoking in
indoor places; it was the first state to do so. Since then,
many countries have banned smoking in public places.
100 And in 2004, the country of Bhutan became the first
country to ban the sale of all tobacco products. The
effectiveness of these bans varies from country to
country. In some places, the bans are virtually ignored,
while in others, such as the United States, the bans are
105 taken very seriously.
    Why do people smoke when they know it is bad for
their health? According to many researchers, smoking is
one of the most difficult habits to break. Mark Twain,
the American writer, once said, "To quit smoking is the
110 easiest thing I ever did; I ought to know because I've
done it hundreds of times."

a Vocabulary

variety	rub	tax	failure
occupied	wound	label	inhale
lung	rites	basically	cultivate

1. It was so cold that I had to _____ my hands together to warm them.

2. In the south, they can grow a _____ of vegetables, not just the few we can _____ here.

3. Every religion has different burial _____.

4. _____ damage can cause serious breathing problems.

5. The _____ on canned food gives information about the ingredients in the food.

6. Tom seems unfriendly, but he's _____ a kind and generous person.

7. When you _____, your chest should expand.

8. Our regular classroom was _____ by another class, so we had to go to a different room.

206

9. The doctor put a large bandage on her leg _____.

10. The car cost $10,000 plus _____.

b   Vocabulary

tax	respiratory	encountered	inhale
honor	failure	widespread	secondhand
leading	post-op	complication	toxic

1. On her walk in the woods, she _____ a large bear.

2. The youngest child in a family often has to wear _____ clothes.

3. Which country is the _____ producer of rice?

4. The first airplane that the Wright brothers built was a _____. It couldn't get off the ground.

5. It is a great _____ to be given an award.

6. A person with _____ problems has trouble breathing.

7. A week after surgery, he went to his doctor for a _____ examination.

8. The only _____ we had on our trip was not being able to find our hotel.

9. Any household cleaners that are _____ must be kept out of reach of children.

10. Destruction from the storm was _____; few houses were left undamaged.

c   Vocabulary Review: Antonyms

Match the antonyms.

_____ 1. deprive   a. degrade

_____ 2. boost   b. provide

_____ 3. enhance   c. wealth

_____ 4. volatile   d. foreign

_____ 5. poverty   e. enter

_____ 6. discord   f. unimportant

_____ 7. native   g. lower

_____ 8. vital   h. accurate

_____ 9. potential   i. agreement

_____ 10. withdraw   j. calm

                               k. achieve

                               l. impossible

d   Comprehension Check: True/False/Not Enough Information

_____ 1. The tobacco plant is native to Asia.

_____ 2. Some Native Americans used tobacco in their religious rites.

_____ 3. The Spanish explorers learned to smoke tobacco, while the Portuguese used tobacco as snuff.

_____ 4. Tobacco wasn't banned until the 1900s.

_____ 5. People have always known that smoking is bad for their health.

_____ 6. In the early 20th century, there was already evidence of a link between smoking and lung cancer.

_____ 7. The tobacco industry can no longer pay filmmakers to show people smoking in their movies.

_____ 8. You don't have to smoke yourself to be affected by cigarette smoke.

_____ 9. Parents who smoke are more likely to have children who smoke.

_____ 10. The children of smokers are more likely to have respiratory problems than are the children of nonsmokers.

208

e   Comprehension Questions

1. What are some of the different ways in which people have used the tobacco plant?
2. What is snuff?
3. Why did the Spanish and Portuguese explorers use tobacco differently?
4. Where was smoking banned in the 17th century?
5. Why didn't governments enforce the smoking ban in the 17th century?
6. How did the U.S. government try to discourage smoking in the 1960s?
7. What did the tobacco industry do to encourage people to smoke?
8. What is secondhand smoke?
9. What effect can smoking have on nonsmokers?
10. In addition to causing lung cancer, what other effects can smoking have on a person's health?
11. What has the government of Bhutan done to discourage people from smoking?

f   Reading Strategy: Distinguishing Facts and Opinions

*Identify each statement below as a fact or an opinion. Write **Fact** or **Opinion** on the line.*

_____ 1. Today, tobacco is grown in roughly 120 countries.

_____ 2. Some people think tobacco can cure toothaches.

_____ 3. Smoking causes lung cancer.

_____ 4. People should quit smoking.

_____ 5. It's important for governments to enforce smoking bans.

_____ 6. Some of the chemicals in tobacco are toxic.

_____ 7. If you have children, you shouldn't smoke.

_____ 8. If you smoke at home, your children are more likely to develop breathing problems.

209

g   Vocabulary Expansion: The Prefix *mis-*

The prefix *mis-* can be added to the beginning of some words to make the meaning negative.

Choose verbs from the list below to complete the sentences that follow. Make any necessary changes to the tense and form of the verbs.

miscalculate	mismanage	mislead	misread
misplace	misbehave	misunderstand	misprint

1. How often do you _____ your keys?
2. Did you _____ a lot when you were a child?
3. If your bank _____ your account balance, what would you do?
4. What is likely to happen to people who _____ their businesses?
5. Many arguments start simply because people _____ each other.
6. She _____ him by saying she enjoyed cooking when she didn't.
7. The newspaper _____ the name of the company but corrected its mistake the next day.
8. I thought it was going to rain today, but I must have _____ the weather forecast in the newspaper.

h   Grammar Review: Prepositions

Write the correct preposition on the line.

The use of tobacco (1) _____ cigarettes didn't become popular until late in the 19th century. Thanks (2) _____ an effective advertising campaign (3) _____ the 1880s, cigarette smoking became widespread. Back then, most people thought that cigarettes helped to relieve tension; they didn't believe that cigarettes were harmful (4) _____ a person's health. (5) _____ the 20th century, however, doctors began seeing an increasing number (6) _____ cases of lung cancer, and (7) _____ 1950 researchers in England reported the first evidence showing a link between smoking and lung cancer. Fourteen years later, (8) _____ 1964, the U.S. Surgeon General announced that smoking causes lung cancer. Soon after that, the first warning labels appeared (9) _____ cigarette packages, and cigarette advertisements were banned (10) _____ television and radio (11) _____ England and the United States. The tobacco industry responded (12) _____ paying filmmakers to show actors and actresses smoking (13) _____ their movies. Fearing that the health warnings would encourage people to stop smoking, cigarette makers also increased the amount of nicotine (14) _____ cigarettes to make them more addictive.

i Sentence Combining

Read the example and the model combinations below. Then rewrite sentences 1 and 2 following the models.

Example: Smoking is unhealthy. It also costs governments billions of dollars in health-care costs.

Models: a. Smoking is unhealthy, and it costs governments billions of dollars in health-care costs.

b. Smoking not only is unhealthy, but also costs governments billions of dollars in health-care costs.

c. Not only is smoking unhealthy; it also costs governments billions of dollars in health-care costs.

1. Smoking is bad for the smoker. It also is harmful to the people nearby.

a. _____

b. _____

c. _____

2. The children of smokers are more likely to have health problems. They also have respiratory problems more often.

a. _____

b. _____

c. _____

j Writing

Advertisements can be very powerful. Write a magazine or television advertisement against smoking. Try to make it interesting to young adults. When you finish, share your ad with your classmates and discuss it.

Memory

lesson

2

© Britt Erlanson/Getty Images

Before You Read

1. Do you think you have a good memory? Why or why not?

2. What things do you often forget? What things are easy for you to remember?

3. What is your oldest memory?

212

Context Clues

*The words in **bold** print below are from this lesson. Use context clues to guess what each word means.*

1. Scientists are still trying to **figure out** exactly what memory is.

2. We do know that a memory is not just one thing stored somewhere in the brain. Instead, a memory is made up of **bits** and pieces of information stored all over the brain.

3. Ask questions when you are trying to learn new information to be **certain** that you understand it accurately.

4. If you **come across** a new word, make a picture in your mind of the word and the thing it represents.

2   Memory

When you say that someone has a good memory, what exactly do you mean? Are you saying that the person has fast <u>recall</u> or that she or he <u>absorbs</u> information quickly? Or maybe you just mean that the
5   person remembers a lot about her or his childhood. The truth is that it is difficult to say exactly what memory is. Even scientists who have been studying memory for decades say that they are still trying to **figure out** exactly what it is. We do know that a <u>particular</u> memory
10   is not just one thing stored somewhere in the brain. Instead, a memory is made up of <u>bits</u> and pieces of information stored all over the brain. Perhaps, then, the best way to describe memory is to say that it is a process—a process of **recording**, storing, and <u>retrieving</u>
15   information. It is this process that allows us to <u>retain</u> memories of past events as well as to remember an unlimited number of facts.

     In order for a piece of information to be remembered, it must first be recorded in the brain. And

Margin notes:

ability to call back something remembered

takes in

specific

small amounts

bringing back

keep

20 to record something in the brain, you have to really
    notice it or register it, using one or more of your five
    senses—sight, hearing, touch, taste, and smell. Practice
    and **repetition** can then help to strengthen the pieces
    that make up your memory of that information.

25   Memory can be negatively affected by a number of
    things. Poor nutrition and **depression** can affect a   **feelings of great**
    person's ability to retain information. **Excessive** alcohol **sadness**
    use can also **impair** memory and cause permanent
    damage to the brain over the long term. A **vision** or
30 hearing impairment may affect a person's ability to
    notice certain things, **thus** making it harder to record   **for that reason**
    information in the brain.

        When people talk about memory, they often refer to
    short-term memory and long-term memory. If you want
35 to call a store or an office that you don't call often, you
    look in the telephone book for the number. You **dial** the
    number, and then you forget it! You use your short-term
    memory to remember the number. Your short-term
    memory lasts about 30 seconds, or half a minute.
40 However, you don't need to look in the telephone book
    for your best friend's number, because you already
    know it. This number is in your long-term memory,
    which stores information about things you have learned
    and experienced through the years.

45   Why do you forget things sometimes? The major
    reason for forgetting something is that you did not learn
    it well enough in the beginning. For example, if you
    meet some new people and right away forget their
    names, it is because you did not register the names
50 when you heard them.

        You can help yourself to remember better. Here are
    some ideas.

    1. Move information from your short-term memory
       to your long-term memory. You can do this by
       practicing the new information. Say it out loud to
       yourself. Think about it.
    2. After you learn something, study it again and
       again. Learn it more than you need to. This process
       is called overlearning. For example, when you

learn new words, practice using them in sentences. Don't try to memorize words only from a list.

3. Make sure that you understand new information. It is difficult to remember something that you don't **comprehend**. Ask questions when you are trying to learn new information to be **certain** that you understand it accurately.

4. Get rid of any **distractions** in the room where you are studying. Do not listen to music or watch television while you are studying. You will remember better if you concentrate on just one thing at a time.

5. Try to connect new information with something that you already know. For example, when you learn the name of a new kind of food, think of a similar kind of food that you are already familiar with.

6. Divide new information into several sections (about five or six). Learn one section at a time, stopping for a few minutes between sections. Don't sit down and try to learn a very large amount of new information **all at once**.

7. Use **visualization techniques** when you are learning new information. For example, if you **come across** a new word, make a picture in your mind of the word and the thing it represents. This **mental** picture will help you remember that word the next time you see or hear it.

8. Think of word clues to help you remember information. One helpful kind of word clue is an acronym. An acronym is an expression formed from the first letters of a group of words. For example, many American schoolchildren learn the names of the Great Lakes in North America by remembering the word *homes*. *Homes* is an acronym that comes from the names of the Great Lakes: *Huron, Ontario, Michigan, Erie, Superior.*

9. Relax when you study! Try to enjoy yourself. You are learning new things every minute. You will remember better if you are happy and relaxed.

215

a Vocabulary

recall	absorb	figure out	particular
bits	retrieve	retain	repetition
depression	excessive	impaired	vision

1. A towel can _____ water, but a piece of metal cannot.
2. If you eat an _____ amount of food, you will gain weight.
3. I wonder why there are _____ of paper all over the floor.
4. No other shirts would please him; he wanted only that _____ shirt.
5. The company tried to _____ all of its employees, but it finally had to let several people leave.
6. Lack of interest in things and feelings of sadness are signs of _____.
7. If you throw a ball to my dog, he will run after it and _____ it.
8. After the fifth _____, he was able to say the poem without looking at his book.
9. I can't _____ if I'm supposed to be there at 3 or 4.
10. If you have _____ vision, you have to wear glasses when you drive a car.
11. Spending a lot of time in front of a computer could harm your _____.
12. How do I _____ the area of a triangle?

b Vocabulary

dial	comprehend	record	excessive
all at once	visualize	technique	came across
mental	certain	thus	distracting

1. So many things happened _____ that we didn't know what to do first.
2. I used a videotape to _____ the graduation ceremony.

3. Could you please stop talking for a minute. You're _____ me.
4. It is hard for me to _____ why anyone would want to live in Antarctica for a whole year.
5. She's not sure she'll be here today, but she's _____ she'll get here tomorrow.
6. Can you _____ the house you would like to live in someday?
7. What do you do when you _____ the wrong telephone number?
8. Do you have a good _____ for remembering phone numbers?
9. I _____ an interesting article while I was doing research on the Internet.
10. Reading and writing are _____ activities.
11. She knew all the answers to the exam questions; _____, she got an A.

C Vocabulary Review: Synonyms

Match the synonyms.

_____ 1. suitable	a. hopeful	
_____ 2. attempt	b. exceptionally	
_____ 3. optimistic	c. appropriate	
_____ 4. primarily	d. fair	
_____ 5. diverse	e. try	
_____ 6. traits	f. think	
_____ 7. impact	g. varied	
_____ 8. extraordinarily	h. sharp	
_____ 9. impartial	i. affect	
_____ 10. ponder	j. mainly	
	k. achieve	
	l. characteristics	

d Comprehension Check: Multiple Choice

Circle the letter of the best answer.

1. A memory is stored in your brain _____.
   a. in one place
   b. in many different places
   c. in a couple of places

2. To record something in your memory, you have to first _____.
   a. retrieve it
   b. retain it
   c. register it

3. Repetition can help to _____ a memory.
   a. lose
   b. impair
   c. strengthen

4. _____ can impair memory.
   a. Drinking alcohol
   b. Using the telephone
   c. Repeating things

5. Short-term memory lasts about _____.
   a. 3 seconds
   b. 30 seconds
   c. half an hour

6. When you learn something, you move it into _____.
   a. short-term memory
   b. long-term memory
   c. both short-term and long-term memory

7. Saying something out loud helps you _____.
   a. hold it in short-term memory
   b. remember it
   c. retrieve it

8. Distractions can _____.
   a. prevent you from concentrating
   b. help you retain information
   c. help you visualize

9. It's not a good idea to try to learn a lot of new things _____.
   a. in sections
   b. over time
   c. all at once

10. When you visualize something, you _____.
    a. look for it
    b. make a mental picture of it
    c. ask questions to make certain you understood correctly

e Comprehension Questions

1. Where are memories stored in the brain?
2. What are memories made up of?
3. What are the three steps in the memory process?
4. What are some things that can harm memory?
5. What is the difference between short-term memory and long-term memory?
6. What is overlearning?
7. What shouldn't you do when you study?
8. How can an acronym help you retrieve information?

Reading Strategy: Identifying Cause and Effect

Complete the chart below with the missing effects.

Cause	Effect
Practice and repetition	
Depression and malnutrition	
Overlearning information	
Distractions in the room where you are studying	
Making a mental picture of a new word	

Vocabulary Expansion: Word Forms

Choose the right word form for each sentence below.

	Verb	Noun	Adjective	Adverb
1.	visualize	visualization	visual	visually
2.	distract	distraction	distracted	distractedly
3.	comprehend	comprehension	comprehensive	comprehensively
4.	absorb	absorption	absorbent	
5.	retrieve	retrieval		
6.		excess	excessive	excessively
7.	impair	impairment	impaired	
8.	repeat	repetition	repetitive repetitious	repetitively
9.	depress	depression	depressed	

1. Can you _____ yourself flying an airplane?
2. Each time the telephone rings, it _____ everyone.
3. Your _____ of the language has increased tremendously.
4. Young children _____ new information at an incredible rate.
5. They used a fishing pole to _____ her ring from the bottom of the lake.
6. I sometimes get a headache when I'm with my best friend because she talks _____.
7. Drinking alcohol can _____ a person's ability to drive.
8. His speech was too _____; he just kept saying the same thing over and over again.
9. The lack of sunlight in the winter seems to _____ him.

h Grammar Review: Noun Substitutes

*Read each sentence or pair of sentences and study the pronoun in **bold** print. Circle the noun or noun phrase that each pronoun replaces.*

1. Practice the new information. Say **it** out loud to yourself.
2. This process is called overlearning. For example, when you learn new words, practice using **them** in sentences.
3. It is difficult to remember something that you don't comprehend. Ask questions when you are trying to learn new information to be certain that you understand **it** accurately.
4. If you come across a new word, make a picture in your mind of the word and the thing **it** represents.
5. The major reason for forgetting something is that you did not learn it well enough in the beginning. For example, if you meet some new people and right away forget their names, it is because you did not register the names when you heard **them**.
6. You don't need to look in the telephone book for your best friend's number, because you already know **it**. This number is in your long-term memory.

i Sentence Combining

Read the example and the model combinations below. Then rewrite sentences 1 and 2 following the models.

Example: Memory is difficult to define. It isn't just one thing.

Models: a. Memory is difficult to define because it isn't just one thing.

   b. Memory, which isn't just one thing, is difficult to define.

   c. Because memory isn't just one thing, it's difficult to define.

1. Excessive alcohol use is bad for your health. It can cause permanent brain damage.

   a. _____
   b. _____
   c. _____

2. Short-term memory is very useful. It holds information while you are using it.

   a. _____

   b. _____

   c. _____

 Writing

Think about one of your best memories. Describe it in a paragraph for your classmates to read.

Obesity: The New Epidemic

© BananaStock/Alamy

Before You Read

1. What were some of the most serious health problems in the past?

2. What are some of the most serious health problems today?

3. What connection can you make between the photograph and the topic of health problems?

Context Clues

The words in **bold** *print below are from this lesson. Use context clues to guess what each word means.*

1. The most serious health problem in the world used to be **infectious** diseases such as typhoid fever and influenza (flu).

2. One cause of the problem is the **sedentary** lifestyle that many people in the 21st century are leading. Getting around by car and working at a desk don't demand much physical activity.

3. The fast-food industry spends over $33 billion a year to attract customers. Agencies created to educate people about healthy eating have only a **fraction** of that amount of money.

3   Obesity: The New Epidemic

ep·i·dem·ic /ˌɛpəˈdɛmɪk/ *n.* a disease that spreads quickly among many people: *There are <n.pl.> epidemics of influenza nearly every winter.*

The most serious health problem in the world used to be **infectious** diseases such as typhoid fever, influenza (flu), and bubonic plague. In the 14th century, for example, an epidemic of bubonic plague killed
5 roughly one-third of the population of Asia and about half of the population of Europe. A flu epidemic in 1918 killed millions of people around the world. Today, however, vaccines and antibiotics have prevented the spread of many serious diseases. In fact, in many parts
10 of the world today, infectious diseases are no longer considered to be the most serious health problem. According to Dr. Julie Gerberding, **director** of the Centers for Disease Control and Prevention (CDC) in the United States, the number one health problem in the
15 United States is the new epidemic of **obesity**.

What does it mean to be obese? Most doctors and researchers use the body mass **index**, or BMI, to **determine** whether someone is **overweight** or obese. The BMI equals a person's weight in kilograms divided
20 by the square of the person's height in meters. A normal BMI is between 18.5 and 24.9. A person with a body mass index of 25.0 to 29.9 is considered to be overweight, while a person with a BMI of 30 or above is said to be obese. It is estimated that roughly 51 percent
25 of the adults in the United States and Canada are either overweight or obese. Worldwide, an estimated 22 million children under the age of five are believed to be overweight.

an indicator

What is causing the epidemic of obesity? One
30 obvious contributing factor is the **sedentary** lifestyle that many people in the 21st century are leading. Getting around by car and working at a desk don't demand much physical activity. "Physical activity used to be what people had to do to survive," says Dr. David
35 Katz, **associate** clinical professor of public health at Yale University. "Now we speak of it as something we have to work into our day."

A second cause of the obesity epidemic is an increase in the availability and consumption of **junk** food. The
40 Centers for Disease Control and Prevention defines junk foods as "foods which **provide** **calories** primarily through fats or added sugars and have **minimal** amounts of vitamins and minerals." Studies have shown that people are consuming **substantially** more
45 calories daily than they used to, and they are consuming many of those calories outside of **regular** meals. **In other words**, people are snacking, or eating between meals, a lot more than they used to, and those snacks often consist of junk food.

units of energy produced by food

very small

a lot

50 The **skyrocketing** popularity of fast-food restaurants over the past 30 years has also contributed to the obesity epidemic. The goal of most fast-food restaurants is to make high profits by producing meals cheaply and efficiently, with little concern for the nutritional content
55 of the food. **Consequently**, much of the food served in

increasing rapidly

as a result

fast-food restaurants is high in saturated fats, sodium, and sugar. The "great taste" of the food comes from artificial **flavorings** created in science laboratories. For example, roughly 50 artificial ingredients are used to
60 make the strawberry milkshake sold in one popular fast-food restaurant. High-quality meat has been replaced by lower-quality meat that is full of preservatives to make it taste good. While the nutritional content of much fast food is declining, the
65 serving sizes have been getting larger, encouraging people to consume more calories.

A study in 2004 provided the first scientific evidence of a link between eating fast food regularly and obesity and obesity-related diseases. The study followed 3,000
70 young people between the ages of 18 and 30 for 15 years. Researchers found that people who ate a fast-food meal at least twice a week were 10 pounds or more heavier than those who ate fast food less than once a week. According to Mark Pereira, who worked on the
75 study, "People really should be taking a hard look at their diet. One simple change that people could make is reducing their frequency of going to fast-food restaurants and eating more at home."

The fast-food industry spends over $33 billion a year
80 to attract customers to its restaurants. Restaurants <u>lure</u> children by offering toys, playgrounds, entertainment, and a party atmosphere. Adults are attracted by the fast service and the predictability of both the food and the environment. Agencies created to educate people about
85 healthy eating have only a **fraction** of that amount of money with which to get their message across.

In 2001, the U.S. Surgeon General reported that obesity can be linked to roughly 300,000 deaths and $117 billion in health-care costs a year. Among the
90 health problems caused by obesity are respiratory difficulties, **deterioration** of bones and muscles, high blood pressure, and skin problems. The more **life-threatening** problems include heart disease, type 2 diabetes, and certain types of cancer. Clearly, something
95 must be done to stop this new epidemic.

lure attract with promises; entice

227

a Vocabulary

infected	lure	flavor	director
obesity	index	determined	overweight
sedentary	regularly	junk	provide

1. A computer programmer has a _____ job, but a farmer does not.
2. What documents do you have to _____ when you enter another country?
3. What is the body mass _____?
4. The head of an agency is sometimes called its _____.
5. If you don't clean a cut, it could become _____.
6. If you are just a little bit _____, it's not a serious problem, though you should probably lose the extra weight as soon as possible.
7. My car is a piece of _____; it doesn't run well at all.
8. To prevent cavities, you should brush your teeth _____.
9. _____ is a growing problem among both children and adults.
10. I _____ from the weight shown on the scale that I needed to go on diet.

b Vocabulary

calories	minimal	substantial	in other words
skyrocketed	flavor	consequently	deteriorate
lure	fraction	associate	life-threatening

1. I ate a _____ of the amount of pizza that he ate.
2. Cream contains more _____ than milk.
3. She eats fast food regularly. _____, she's a fast-food junkie.
4. In just one week, the price of eggs _____ from $2.00 to $8.00.
5. There is a _____ amount of sugar in the tea. I don't think you will even notice it.
6. I brush my teeth regularly. _____, I have no cavities.

7. She used a piece of meat to _____ her dog back into the house.

8. What is your favorite ice cream _____?

9. When he stopped drinking soda and eating junk food, he lost 20 kilos. That's a _____ amount of weight.

10. Some fast food is so full of preservatives that it won't _____.

11. My _____ and I run the business together.

12. The _____ problems he was experiencing were a direct result of obesity.

C Vocabulary Review: Definitions

Match the words with their definitions.

_____ 1. all at once
_____ 2. retain
_____ 3. fragile
_____ 4. exploit
_____ 5. fantasy
_____ 6. monitor
_____ 7. off-limits
_____ 8. transmit

a. easily damaged
b. dream
c. send
d. watch carefully over time
e. feeling of togetherness
f. not open to visitors
g. keep; hold on to
h. suddenly
i. staff
j. take advantage of; treat unfairly

d Comprehension Check: True/False/Not Enough Information

_____ 1. Infectious diseases are a more serious problem today than in the past.

_____ 2. *BMI* stands for body mass index.

_____ 3. Doctors can use the BMI to determine whether someone is underweight.

_____ 4. To determine your BMI, you need to know your weight only.

_____ 5. The number of obese people in the world will double in the next 10 years.

Lesson 3: Obesity: The New Epidemic

_____ 6. People are more sedentary now than in the past.

_____ 7. Junk food provides few calories.

_____ 8. Much fast food contains artificial flavoring and preservatives.

_____ 9. There is no scientific evidence that eating fast food regularly can cause obesity.

_____10. The fast-food industry is willing to spend a lot of money to get people to eat their food.

e Comprehension Questions

1. Why do some people call obesity an epidemic?
2. How is the epidemic of obesity different from epidemics in the past?
3. What is the body mass index of a person of normal weight?
4. Would a person with a BMI of 31 be considered overweight or obese?
5. Why do you think so many children are obese today?
6. What is junk food?
7. How have people's eating habits changed in the last 20 years?
8. Why aren't fast-food restaurants more concerned about serving healthy food?
9. Why is it possible for fast-food restaurants to use lower-quality meats?
10. What are some of the health effects of being overweight or obese?

f Reading Strategy: Distinguishing Fact and Opinion

Identify each statement below as a fact or an opinion. Write **Fact** _or_ **Opinion** _on the line. Then underline the words in the sentence that help you to know it is a fact or an opinion._

_____ 1. The 1918 flu epidemic killed millions of people.

_____ 2. Julie Gerberding works for the Centers for Disease Control and Prevention.

_____ 3. Dr. Gerberding thinks that obesity is the most serious health problem in the United States today.

_____ 4. The BMI provides a good way to determine whether someone is overweight.

_____ 5. Physical activity used to be what people had to do to survive.

_____ 6. People eat a lot more junk food today than they did 20 years ago.

_____ 7. In 2001, the U.S. Surgeon General reported that obesity can be linked to roughly 300,000 deaths a year.

_____ 8. People should be looking hard at their diet.

g Vocabulary Expansion: Collocations

Match the verbs and nouns you can use together. Write the number of one or more verbs next to each noun.

Verbs	Nouns
1. absorb	_____ a. information
2. inhale	_____ b. surgery
3. lead	_____ c. someone's name
4. memorize	_____ d. calories
5. dial	_____ e. water
6. perform	_____ f. a horse
7. recall	_____ g. a list of words
8. consume	_____ h. smoke
	_____ i. a sedentary lifestyle
	_____ j. a number
	_____ k. fuel
	_____ l. a task

h Grammar Review: Transition Words

Choose a transition word from the list to complete each sentence below.

nevertheless	in spite of	even though
in fact	in other words	consequently

1. Obesity is becoming a serious problem among young children. _____, more than 22 million children are now thought to be overweight.

2. People need to consume fewer calories and engage in more physical activity. _____, they need to eat less and exercise more.

3. People know that a lot of fast food is very unhealthy. _____, they still want to eat it.

Lesson 3: Obesity: The New Epidemic

4. _____ the high amount of sodium and fat in fast food, many people eat it several times a week.

5. Some people eat a lot of fast food _____ they know it isn't good for them.

6. Restaurants are serving larger and larger portions of food. _____, customers are consuming more calories than they used to.

Sentence Combining

Read the example and the model combinations below. Then rewrite sentences 1 and 2 following the models.

Example: Fast-food companies lure children to their restaurants. They offer toys and a party atmosphere.

Models:
a. Fast-food companies lure children to their restaurants by offering toys and a party atmosphere.

b. By offering toys and a party atmosphere, fast-food companies lure children to their restaurants.

c. To lure children to their restaurants, fast-food companies offer toys and a party atmosphere.

1. Fast-food companies make high profits. They produce meals cheaply and efficiently.

a. _____
b. _____
c. _____

2. Doctors can determine whether someone is overweight. They use the body mass index.

a. _____
b. _____
c. _____

Writing

Think about your eating habits and decide whether you have good eating habits or poor eating habits. Then explain in writing why you think so. Include details and examples in your writing.

lesson 4

Can Fashion Be Hazardous to Your Health?

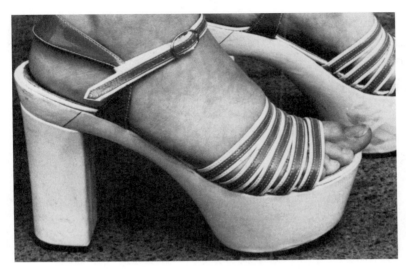

© Tim Graham/Getty Images

Before You Read

1. How might the shoes in the photo be harmful to a person's health?

2. What are some other examples of popular clothes that are either uncomfortable or dangerous to wear?

3. What are some common things that men and women do to look more attractive?

Context Clues

*The words in **bold** print below are from this lesson. Use context clues to guess what each word means.*

1. Just because something is popular, or **fashionable,** doesn't mean that it is going to be good for your health.

2. History is full of examples of unhealthy things people have been willing to do in the name of fashion, and today there are still many people who risk their health just to be **in style**.

3. In the 16th century, many women put white **makeup** on their faces to be fashionable.

4. At other times in history, women were willing to drink small amounts of the poison arsenic because it made them look fashionably **pale**.

4   Can Fashion Be Hazardous to Your Health?

Just because something is popular, or **fashionable,** doesn't mean that it is going to be good for your health. History is full of examples of unhealthy things people have been willing to do in the name of fashion,
5   and today there are still many people who risk their health just to be **in style**.

    Many people are familiar with the neck ring custom of the Padaung people of Myanmar. At about age five, young girls begin to wear their first rings, which can
10   weigh as much as 3 kilograms; over time, more rings are added. The weight of the rings pushes down the young girl's collarbone and upper ribs, making the neck appear to be very long. Unfortunately, the rings also cause the muscles of the neck to become so **weak**
15   that they can no longer hold up the head. If the neck

rings were removed, the woman would not be able to sit or stand up.

    The ancient Chinese practice of foot **binding** is another example of beauty at the price of health. This

20 very painful **procedure** began when a young girl was between the ages of three and six. During the procedure, the four smaller toes on each foot were broken and turned under, and the feet were **wrapped** tightly with a **bandage**. Each day, the bandage was

25 tightened a little more to make the foot smaller and smaller. After several years, the child's feet were just 8 to 10 centimeters long, making it impossible for her to walk naturally. The procedure itself was hazardous, with perhaps as many as 10 percent of the girls dying

30 from infection or circulation problems caused by the tight bandages.

    While the binding of feet might seem **absurd** to us today, women continue to do damage to their feet in the name of beauty. Wearing high heels, for example,

35 shortens the muscles of the lower leg and can cause the back to **arch** unnaturally. This can lead to serious back problems and **nerve** damage. When **ultra**-high platform shoes were popular in Japan, police officials **accused** them of causing many car accidents. They said that

40 the thick **soles** of the shoes slowed the response time of drivers, especially when they had to **brake** in an emergency.

    Cosmetics have been in use for thousands of years, and while many types of cosmetics are harmless, there

45 are some that can be dangerous **indeed**. In the 16th century, for example, white skin was the **ideal**, and many women put white **makeup** on their faces to be in style. Unfortunately, the makeup was made with the poisonous metals lead and mercury. Used over a long

50 period of time, the makeup could eventually remove layers of skin, cause teeth to fall out, and sometimes poison people, leading to death. At other times in history, women were willing to drink small amounts of the poison arsenic because it made them look

50 fashionably **pale**.

---

tying tightly

method (for doing something)

covered

curve

extremely; very

bottoms

stop or slow down

truly

goal; idea of perfection

The popularity of corsets in Europe in the 16th century provided another opportunity for women to exchange health for beauty. A corset is a tight-fitting piece of clothing that women wore to change the shape

55 of their body. Made of steel, leather, and bone, corsets were supposed to provide every woman with the tiny **waist** that was so fashionable at the time. Unfortunately, corsets were also known to break ribs, **puncture** lungs, cause indigestion, and bring on shortness of breath. In

60 fact, when corsets became popular again in the 19th century, a new type of furniture known as a fainting couch became popular as well. A fainting couch looked like a narrow bed, but it was placed in sitting rooms and other public places. At a time when women

65 frequently **fainted** because of their tight-fitting corsets, it was useful to have a **convenient** place for them to lie down.

middle section of a person's body

passed out; lost consciousness

easy to use or get to

While corsets are not fashionable today, there is no shortage of hazardous things that people are willing to

70 do to be in style. In some parts of the world, people are willing to pay for a procedure known as leg stretching just to become 8 centimeters taller. This procedure involves breaking the leg bones and then slowly, over a period of months, stretching the legs. The risks include

75 nerve damage, bones becoming too weak to support the body, and uneven legs. Lying out in the sun to change the color of your skin is still a popular activity in many parts of the world, despite the fact that too much sun can cause skin cancer. Body **piercing** has been a custom

80 in many parts of the world for centuries, but now we know about some of the health risks that go along with this fashion. Piercing the skin can cause infection, and piercing the tongue can cause gum damage and even broken teeth.

85 Throughout history, people have done extraordinary things to their bodies just to be fashionable. Pain, medical complications, and even the risk of death have not discouraged people from trying to become more beautiful.

a Vocabulary

fashionable	bind	procedure	bandage
absurd	arch	nerves	ultra
accused	soles	brake	weak

1. Has anyone ever _____ you of doing something you didn't do?
2. High divers often _____ their backs when they are up in the air.
3. Corsets used to be _____, but they no longer are.
4. What is the _____ for getting a passport in your country?
5. What can you use to _____ several sticks together?
6. When you want to stop a car, you have to step on the _____.
7. It seems _____ to do something that could harm your health.
8. _____ carry messages from your brain to different parts of your body.
9. The skin on the _____ of your feet is harder than the skin on your arms.
10. A very light airplane is called an _____ -light.
11. A _____ helps to protect a wound by keeping it clean.

b Vocabulary

in style	wrap	indeed	ideal
makeup	pale	waist	puncture
faint	convenient	pierced	weak

1. Another word for *cosmetics* is _____.
2. Everyone thought she was sick because she looked very _____.
3. If you think you are going to _____, you should sit down.

Lesson 4: Can Fashion Be Hazardous to Your Health?

4. He _____ the meat with a fork to see if it was cooked completely.
5. It costs a lot of money to be _____ all of the time.
6. If you want to touch your toes with your legs straight, you have to bend at the _____.
7. Different cultures have different definitions of the _____ parent or the _____ husband or wife.
8. If you _____ a tire on your bicycle, all the air will escape.
9. In some cultures, people _____ a cloth around their head.
10. Did I have a good trip? _____ I did.
11. Driving a car is more _____ than taking a bus, but it is more wasteful too.
12. Her knees felt _____, and she began to fall to the floor.

c Vocabulary Review: Odd One Out

Circle the word that doesn't fit in each group.

1. extremely, significantly, foolishly, dramatically
2. figure out, determine, identify, emit
3. deteriorate, designate, worsen, degrade
4. devote, impair, damage, harm
5. absurd, strange, bizarre, regular
6. accuse, blame, encounter, suspect
7. accelerate, brake, slow down, stop
8. catastrophe, drought, epidemic, impression

d Comprehension Check: True/False/Not Enough Information

_____ 1. Most fashionable things are hazardous.
_____ 2. The Padaung women who wear neck rings frequently take them off.
_____ 3. Neck rings help the muscles to become stronger.
_____ 4. All Chinese women had their feet bound.

         5.   The pain from foot binding lasted for only a short time.

         6.   High heels aren't good for a person's back.

         7.   Most cosmetics used to be poisonous.

         8.   Only women used to wear corsets.

         9.   Piercing the tongue is very painful.

        10.   Leg stretching is a relatively painless procedure.

e Comprehension Questions

1. How can neck rings be dangerous to a person's health?
2. What health problems could foot binding cause?
3. What is unhealthy about wearing high heels?
4. Why is it dangerous to drive while you are wearing platform shoes?
5. Why did women in the 16th century want to have white skin?
6. Why did corsets become fashionable?
7. How could a corset damage a person's health?
8. What was the purpose of a fainting couch?
9. What are the health risks of leg stretching?
10. What other fashions may be hazardous to a person's health?

Reading Strategy: Taking Notes in a Chart

Use the chart below to take notes on the information in the text on pages 234–236.

Paragraph	Main idea	Important details
2 (lines 7–17)	The custom of wearing neck rings is dangerous to a person's health.	The rings push down the collarbone and upper ribs. The neck muscles become too weak to hold up the head.
3 (lines 18–31)		
4 (lines 32–42)		
5 (lines 43–50)		
6 (lines 51–67)		

g Vocabulary Expansion: Word Forms

Choose the right word form for each sentence below.

	Verb	Noun	Adjective	Adverb
1.		convenience	convenient	conveniently
2.	accuse	accusation	accusative	accusatively
3.	fashion	fashion	fashionable	fashionably
4.		absurdity	absurd	absurdly
5.	idealize	ideal	ideal	ideally
6.	poison	poison	poisonous	
7.	appear	appearance		
8.	circulate	circulation	circulatory	

1. What time would it be _____ for me to come over.
2. Why might someone make a false _____?
3. Are you usually dressed _____?
4. What is the biggest fashion _____ around today?
5. Why do a lot of people _____ tall, thin people?
6. How can parents keep _____ away from their children?
7. What is the most absurd thing you have ever done to your _____?
8. What effect can very cold weather have on your _____?

h Grammar Review: Verb Tense

Complete the paragraph with the correct form of the verb to be.

Cosmetics _____ in use for thousands of years, and while many types of cosmetics _____ harmless, there _____ some that can be dangerous indeed. In the 16th century, for example, white skin _____ the ideal, and many women put white makeup on their faces to be in style. Unfortunately, the makeup _____ made with the poisonous metals

241

lead and mercury. Used over a long period of time, the makeup could eventually remove layers of skin, cause teeth to fall out, and sometimes poison people, leading to death. At other times in history, women _____ willing to drink small amounts of the poison arsenic because it made them look fashionably pale.

i Sentence Combining

Read the example and the model combinations below. Then rewrite sentences 1 and 2 following the models.

Example: Lying out in the sun is still a popular activity. People do it even though they know it can cause cancer.

Models:
a. Lying out in the sun is still a popular activity, even though people know it can cause cancer.

b. Even though people know that lying out in the sun can cause cancer, it's still a popular activity.

c. Despite the fact that lying out in the sun can cause cancer, it's still a popular activity.

1. Leg stretching is popular in some parts of the world. People do it even though they know it can be dangerous.

a. _____

b. _____

c. _____

2. A lot of women continue to wear high heels. They do it even though they know it can cause back problems.

a. _____

b. _____

c. _____

j Writing

Think of something that is both fashionable and harmful in some way to your health. Describe the fashion, and explain why you think it is unhealthy.

Video Highlights

a Before You Watch

1. You are going to watch a video about a ban on smoking in public places. Such a ban would mean that people could not smoke in restaurants or bars.

   a. What would be your reaction to the ban?
   b. What do you think some of the arguments for and against the ban will be?

2. The words below are used in the video. Look up the words in a dictionary. How do you think these words will be used in the video? In pairs, discuss your ideas.

   advocates   right (to do something)   equivalent
   address (an issue)   business boomed   exposed (to
   addicted   adjustable   something)

b As You Watch

1. Watch the video and listen for the vocabulary words above. How are the words used?

2. Watch the video again. Match the quotes with the people who said them.

   _____ Restaurant patron #1   _____ Chuck Hunt

   _____ Restaurant owner   _____ Bartender

   _____ Mayor   _____ Restaurant patron #2

   a. "You don't have a right to hurt others."

   b. "It's kind of unfair to punish people when you get 'em— you get people addicted to something."

   c. "A total ban is telling us we have to now be the smoking police and tell our customers that they can't do something in our restaurant."

   d. "It affected it [the business] in the beginning, but people seemed to be more adjustable after a period of time."

e. "Most restaurants out here have outside patios, so people have a choice of sitting inside or outside."

f. "I went to Florida, and they didn't have it there. And it was disgusting."

C After You Watch

1. Read the statements. Circle *Agree* or *Disagree* to indicate your opinion about the statements.

   a. The video presents only one side of the issue.

      Agree   Disagree

   b. All bartenders want the ban so that they won't have to inhale secondhand smoke.

      Agree   Disagree

   c. Restaurant owners are worried about how the ban will affect their business.

      Agree   Disagree

   d. Two states have already banned smoking, and businesses have not suffered.

      Agree   Disagree

   e. The restaurant patrons who were interviewed are in favor of the smoking ban.

      Agree   Disagree

2. Form two teams to debate the topic "Should smoking be banned from restaurants and bars?" One team should represent a group of restaurant/bar owners. The other team should represent a group of anti-smoking advocates. First, write down your arguments in the chart below.

Arguments against the ban	Arguments for the ban

Then debate the issue with someone from the other team.

Crossword Puzzle

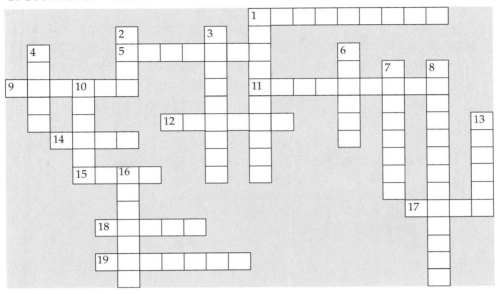

Across

1. Farmers in many places have begun to _____ tobacco crops.
5. Something _____ is a mystery.
9. You can _____ tobacco by smoking cigarettes or through your nose with snuff.
11. too much
12. to hold on to something
14. Potato chips, French fries, cookies, and ice cream are ____ food.
15. Ask for extension 603 after you ____ the number.
17. very light in color
18. poisonous
19. _____ can lead to a variety of health problems, such as type 2 diabetes.

Down

1. I live in a _____ neighborhood, close to the grocery store, laundromat, and subway.
2. Hunters may use food to _____ animals into traps.
3. makeup
4. To be awarded the Nobel Prize is a great _____.
5. Many people wear contact lenses to correct poor _____.
6. Tongue _____ can cause infections and broken teeth.
7. Working on a computer all day can cause vision _____.
10. ridiculous
13. Until recently, infectious diseases and _____ were the biggest health concerns in most countries.
16. sucks up, like a sponge

Dictionary Page

Understanding Labels: Slang

Labels are sometimes placed after the part of speech to give additional information about a word. Look at the label for the adjective *hip*. Slang words are words that are commonly used informally but are considered unacceptable in formal speech and writing.

> **hip** /hɪp/ *n.* **1** the part of the body where the leg joins the pelvis: *He fell and hurt his hip.* **2** the area around the hip joint: *She has wide hips.* *-adj.* (slang) informed, aware, esp. of youthful fashions: *Hey, man, that guy is really hip!*
>
> label

1. Use your dictionary to find the definitions of the following words about fashion.

Word	Definition
1. hip (slang)	*informed, aware, especially of youthful fashions*
2. trendy	
3. old-fashioned	
4. cool (slang)	
5. bad (slang)	
6. frumpy	

2. Look at the photos. With a partner, use the words above to describe the photos.

© Eric Sugita/CORBIS

© Photodisc Collection/Getty Images

© Welsey/Getty Images

Vocabulary

249

incredibly 17
indeed 235
indestructible 15
index 226
infectious 225
infertile 104
influx 105
inhaled 204
inhospitable 103
intermediary 88
invaluable 152
invertebrates 124
issues 56

jail 17
judges 87
junk 226

labels 205
ladder 25
landscape 4
leading 205
lifespan 153
life-threatening 227
link 124
livestock 115
lung 205
lure 227
lush 113

magnificent 134
mainly 4
maintaining 55
makeup 235
malnutrition 77
management 115
massive 137
materials 15
meant 26
mental 215
merge 114
messengers 164
military 152
millennia 27
minimal 226
missionaries 105
missions 55
mobility 176
modified 188
monitor 152
moved (*adj*) 26
murdered 66

native 104
naturalists 135
navigation 152
negotiated 55
nerve 235

nevertheless 187
noticed 25
nutritious 188

obesity 225
occupying 205
off-limits 103
one-on-one 5
optimistic 187
orbits 152
original 6
origins 165
overweight 226
overwhelming 77

p

pale 235
particles 164
particular 213
peak 176
pedestrians 176
penalty 66
peninsula 124
periodic 165
persist 76
pests 188
pesticides 137
philosophy 87
piercing 236
pondered 88
possession 15
post-op 205

potentially 152
poverty 188
prescription 188
presence 39
preserved 26
primarily 164
prison 65
procedure 235
profile 66
promised 6
properly 5
provide 226
publicity 66
puncture 236
punishments 17
purposes 16

r

ratio 5
recall 213
reclaim 115
recognize 87
recording 213
referees 87
refugees 116
registers 136
regular 226
release 65
reliability 66
remarks 65
repaired 154
repetition 214
representatives 54
require 5
resistant 17

251

Matching, 29, 58, 69, 80, 107, 117, 127, 144, 156, 167, 170, 171, 191, 197, 208, 217, 229, 231, 243–244

Multiple-choice questions, 21, 30, 31, 69–70, 80–81, 92, 118, 128–129, 139–140, 168–169, 191–192, 218–219

Odd one out, 41, 90, 138–139, 179, 238

True/false/not enough information questions, 9, 19, 42, 58–59, 91, 108, 127–128, 157, 179, 208, 219–220, 238–239

TOPICS

Art, 1–51
    Cave paintings, 24–35
    Ceramics, 13–23
    Graffiti, 36–45
    Navajo sand painting, 2–12
Health and well-being, 201–247
    Fashions harmful to health, 233–242
    Memory, 212–223
    Obesity, 224–232
    Smoking, 202–211
Organizations, 51–100
    Amnesty International, 63–73
    Olympic Games, 85–95
    UNICEF, 74–84
    United Nations, 52–62
Places, 101–148
    Antarctica, 122–132
    Deserts, 112–121
    Hawaii, 102–111
    National parks, 133–143
Science and technology, 149–200
    Comets, 162–173
    Motor vehicles, 173–183

New plants, 184–196
Satellites, 150–161

VIDEO HIGHLIGHTS, 46–47, 96–97, 144–145, 197–198, 243–244

VIEWING

Group activities, 47, 145
Paintings, 24
Photographs, 2, 36, 63, 233, 248
Videos, 46–47, 96–97, 144–145, 197–198, 243–244

WRITING

Advertisement, 211
Charts, 10, 43, 59, 100, 111, 132, 148, 158, 161, 180, 198, 220, 240, 244, 295
    Timelines, 109
Description, 23, 84, 95, 111, 143, 172, 223, 242
Explanation, 23, 183, 232
Group activities, 97, 211
Ideas, 62
Information, 161
Journal entries, 35
Letters, 73
Lists, 97
Note taking, 10, 71, 96–97, 240
Opinion, 196
Paragraphs, 12, 45, 121
Partner activities, 12, 183
Sentence combining, 12, 22–23, 34–35, 45, 62, 73, 84, 95, 110–111, 121, 131–132, 142–143, 161, 172, 182–183, 196, 211, 222–223, 232, 242
Sentences, 9, 160

Skills Index